Pathfinder®Guides

West Sussex & the South Downs

Walks

Compiled by
Nick Channer

Text: Nick Channer (2010 edition), including some revisions of
                       original text supplied for *PFG More Sussex* and *PFG
                       Surrey and Sussex* by Brian Conduit, John Brooks, David
                       Hancock and Kevin Borman
Photography: Nick Channer, David Hancock and Crimson Publishing
Editor: Ark Creative (UK) Ltd
Designer: Ark Creative (UK) Ltd

OS Ordnance Survey®
Certified Partner

ISBN: 978-1-85458-508-0

While every care has been taken to ensure the accuracy of the route directions,
the publishers cannot accept responsibility for errors or omissions, or for
changes in details given. The countryside is not static: hedges and fences can
be removed, field boundaries can alter, footpaths can be rerouted and changes
in ownership can result in the closure or diversion of some concessionary
paths. Also, paths that are easy and pleasant for walking in fine conditions
may become slippery, muddy and difficult in wet weather, while stepping
stones across rivers and streams may become impassable.

If you find an inaccuracy in either the text or maps, please write to Crimson
Publishing at the address below.

Printed in Singapore. 1/10

First published in Great Britain 2010 by Crimson Publishing,
a division of:
Crimson Business Ltd,
Westminster House, Kew Road, Richmond, Surrey, TW9 2ND

www.totalwalking.co.uk

A catalogue record for this book is available from the British library.

Front cover: Looking out over the Arun Valley
Previous page: Horsted Keynes church

Contents

Approximate walk times

Up to 2½ hours
Short walks on generally clear paths

3–3½ hours
Slightly harder walks of moderate length

4 hours and over
Longer walks including some steep ascents/descents, occasionally on faint paths

The walk times are provided as a guide only and are calculated using an average walking speed of 2½mph (4km/h), adding one minute for each 10m (33ft) of ascent, and then rounding the result to the nearest half hour.

Walks are considered to be dog friendly unless specified.

Walk	Page	Start	Nat. Grid Reference	Distance	Time	Height Gain
Amberley and Parham House	63	Kithurst Hill car park	TQ 070124	7¾ miles (12.4km)	4 hrs	805ft (245m)
Ardingly Reservoir	32	Ardingly Reservoir car park	TQ 335287	5 miles (8km)	2½ hrs	490ft (150m)
Arundel Park and South Stoke	54	Arundel	TQ 020070	7¼ miles (11.6km)	3½ hrs	625ft (190m)
Belloc's Mill	48	Shipley	TQ 143219	6 miles (9.7km)	3 hrs	180ft (55m)
Bignor Hill and the River Arun	88	Bignor Hill	SU 973129	11½ miles (18.4km)	5½ hrs	1,230ft (375m)
Bosham & Fishbourne from West Itchenor	73	West Itchenor	SU 798012	10 miles (16km)	4½ hrs	n/a
Bramber, Beeding and the Downs Link	80	Bramber Castle	TQ 185106	11 miles (17.6km)	5 hrs	295ft (90m)
Chidham Peninsula	34	Chidham	SU 793034	5 miles (8km)	2½ hrs	n/a
Cissbury and Chanctonbury Rings	84	Coombe Rise car park	TQ 133066	11 miles (17.6km)	5½ hrs	1,360ft (415m)
Climping Beach and the River Arun	18	Climping Beach car park	TQ 006008	3¾ miles (6km)	2 hrs	n/a
Cuckfield and Ansty	36	Cuckfield	TQ 304246	5¼ miles (8.4km)	2½ hrs	540ft (165m)
Devil's Dyke	24	Devil's Dyke Hotel	TQ 258110	3¾ miles (6km)	2½ hrs	655ft (200m)
Durford Heath and Rogate Common	12	Durford Heath NT car park	SU 790259	3½ miles (5.6km)	2 hrs	425ft (130m)
Goodwood and the West Sussex Literary Trail	76	Counter's Gate, Goodwood	SU 897113	9½ miles (15.2km)	4½ hrs	1,065ft (325m)
Horsted Keynes and the Bluebell Railway	29	Horsted Keynes railway station	TQ 371292	5 miles (8km)	2½ hrs	475ft (145m)
Kingley Vale	14	West Stoke	SU 824088	3½ miles (5.6km)	2 hrs	475ft (145m)
Loxwood and the Wey South Path	26	Visitor car park, Loxwood	TQ 042311	4½ miles (7.2km)	2 hrs	150ft (45m)
Midhurst and Cowdray Park	45	Midhurst	SU 887217	6½ miles (10.5km)	3 hrs	510ft (155m)
Pulborough Brooks	16	Pulborough	TQ 053185	3¾ miles (6km)	2 hrs	180ft (55m)
Selsey and Pagham Harbour	51	Selsey	SZ 865933	7½ miles (12.1km)	3 hrs	n/a
South Harting to the Downs	66	Harting Downs, off the B2141	SU 789181	7¾ miles (12.4km)	4 hrs	1,130ft (345m)
St Leonard's Forest	22	Roosthole car park	TQ 208297	4 miles (6.4km)	2 hrs	375ft (115m)
The Temple of the Winds from Fernhurst	57	Fernhurst	SU 896284	6¼ miles (10km)	3½ hrs	1,000ft (305m)
Three Commons Walk	20	Iping Common car park	SU 852220	4 miles (6.4km)	2 hrs	330ft (100m)
West Hoathly and Weir Wood Reservoir	69	Finchefield car park	TQ 366325	8 miles (12.9km)	4 hrs	900ft (275m)
The Wey and Arun Canal from Billingshurst	42	Billingshurst library	TQ 085260	6 miles (9.7km)	3 hrs	150ft (45m)
Wolstonbury from Hurstpierpoint	39	Hurstpierpoint	TQ 281165	5¾ miles (9.2km)	3 hrs	670ft (205m)
Woolbeding Common and Hammer Wood	60	Woolbeding Common	SU 869260	7¼ miles (11.6km)	3½ hrs	985ft (300m)

Comments

Parham House is the centrepiece of this spectacular walk which follows a fine stretch of the South Downs Way, offering constant, uninterrupted views in all directions.

Part of the reservoir is used for water sports and may be noisy in summer, but the route leads away from this area to more peaceful countryside, crossing a wonderful footbridge by a nature reserve.

The outward route lies through the splendid park of Arundel Castle while the return follows the meanderings of the River Arun, which provides a fine foreground for views of the romantic stronghold.

Hilaire Belloc lived at Shipley and wrote eloquently about the scenery of Sussex. The walk passes through countryside that he knew and loved and uses field paths and tracks.

This varied walk offers downland, riverside and woodland routes; both the longer options include a choice of pubs.

Make sure that the ferry is operating when you start this walk at West Itchenor. There are no gradients on this coastal walk but *it is possible to get wet boots at Bosham if the tide is exceptionally high.*

Ruined Bramber Castle and Charles II's escape route form a fascinating history to this attractive walk, which follows the River Adur upstream and then across country to the village of Henfield

Avoid this walk at high tide as part of the route is along the tideline. Birdwatchers will enjoy seeing migrants and native waders on the vast, seemingly infinite, mudflats of Chichester Harbour.

Plenty of open and exhilarating walking across the South Downs, with visits to two impressive prehistoric hill forts.

A pleasant, breezy walk offering a rare opportunity to see how nature has shaped an unusually open and undeveloped stretch of Sussex coastline.

From one of the county's loveliest and least spoiled villages, the walk ultimately reaches another rare gem, Cuckfield Park. Along the way are delightful views towards the South Downs.

An excellent introduction to a popular area, this walk begins with a steep descent and ends with a demanding climb. In between the way lies on field paths that skirt two attractive villages.

Much of the sandy soil of the heath is covered with woodland but you emerge into open country before returning via Rogate Common.

The South Downs are famous for their bare hills and open downland. This glorious walk follows downland tracks and a section of the South Downs Way through thickly wooded country.

Preserved steam trains on the charming Bluebell Railway chug merrily beside the path initially, which eventually reaches a delightful lake and the grave of a famous British Prime Minister.

Much of this walk follows a trail around what is alleged to be the finest remaining yew forest in Europe.

A gentle stroll across flat farmland brings the walk to the route of the Sussex Border Path and then the towpath of a disused canal which is gradually being given a new lease of life.

Mainly level – but never dull – walking takes you through woodland and the parkland surrounding the great Tudor palace of Cowdray, which has stood in ruins since a fire in 1793.

Explore the banks of the glorious River Arun on this fascinating, easy walk which takes in a nature reserve and its visitor centre before stepping back in time to look at a church with a fascinating history.

Haunting Pagham Harbour is at the midway point, where there is the chance to visit a largely undiscovered 13th-century chapel by the marshes.

Visit the sizeable village of South Harting near the start of this impressive downland walk before crossing open country to reach the South Downs Way. The return leg is physically demanding but rewarding.

A short and pleasant walk through woodland that passes one of the many hammer ponds of the Sussex Weald.

This walk demands navigational skills and energy, with a height gain of 1,000ft (305m) from the start to the summit of Black Down. The way down is even steeper, and streams often run down the paths.

Good walking on sandy paths takes in Trotton and Stedham Commons, and the route also follows the Rother for a short way.

A great deal of variety is packed into this glorious walk – including stretches of the High Weald Landscape Trail and the Sussex Border Path. Steam trains on the Bluebell Railway make for a sense of nostalgia.

Once across the bypass at Billingshurst, the route enters lovely countryside where you are unlikely to meet other walkers. The stretches by the canal and river offer opportunities to see kingfishers.

Field paths predominate in this excursion, and good breath is needed to climb Wolstonbury, the site of a prehistoric hillfort. There is a good view of Danny, a Tudor mansion, on the return.

Blending airy heath with shady forest, this is another Wealden route that demands wayfaring skills and where mud may be a problem. *Note the warning in the introduction to the walk.*

Introduction to
West Sussex & the South Downs

Artists who produced railway posters in the 1930s were fond of depicting a hiking couple striding along a crest of the South Downs, the man smoking a pipe and swinging a hefty stick, the woman carrying a map and haversack. They tread on springy turf below a blue sky, and you can almost hear a choir of skylarks singing overhead.

The face of West Sussex has changed greatly in the 75 or so years since these posters, but the image created by the railway artist survives in the minds of walkers. Those who explore the South Downs Way will know of favourite stretches where there is still a carpet of turf underfoot, skylarks sing and butterflies rise, heavy with nectar, from wayside flowers. Yet even the most ardent West Sussex supporter has to admit that there are less attractive sections where sheep pastures have been ploughed up and sown with cereals or rapeseed. Here the going may be along a hedgeless, flinty track or, even worse, on a concrete farm road running between vast fields and laid as straight as though the Romans had made it. Fortunately, there remains much more to satisfy than dismay, and it is only older walkers who will remember the South Downs before the 1970s, when the modern pattern of agriculture began in the county.

There are quite a few places in the open countryside of West Sussex where you can look around from high ground and see no evidence of human habitation. An expert looking at the scene, however, would probably spot that 3,000 years ago a fortified settlement occupied a ridge on the horizon or that the muddy ponds on the far side of a field in the middle distance are the remains of a moat that surrounded an early medieval manor house. The Romans also favoured the South Downs and built a number of villas on the sunny, south-facing slopes. They established Chichester as their headquarters and built a road across Sussex to link it with London; parts of this route (Stane Street) have been converted into modern roads but some sections survive as a footpath, especially the highly attractive and scenic stretch that climbs from near Eartham on to the crest of the South Downs at Bignor Hill.

Usually the evidence of human activity is obvious – a compact village lying in the lee of the downs, thatched cottages huddling around an ancient church or an isolated barn built 200 years ago that has recently been expensively converted into a weekend retreat. The domestic architecture of the county is surely one of its most memorable treasures. In towns and villages there is a diversity of style in house and cottage unmatched elsewhere in the kingdom. A medieval timber-framed cottage, with its thatched roof and exposed beams, can be flanked by a weather-boarded house of the 1830s on one side and a slightly later pantiled cottage on the other. Elsewhere in the same street, there may well be handsome Georgian and Regency houses standing close to modern, architect-designed developments.

A wealth of beautiful churches provides another valuable legacy. Important for their historical and architectural interest, they also enhance the scenery of the county. However, a church does not have to be of great age to play its

The Shepherd & Dog at Devil's Dyke

part in the landscape. A tower and a red roof in a vista features in many a watercolour on view in the county's galleries. Visitors will also enjoy seeing grander buildings such as Chichester Cathedral or the fairytale façade of Arundel Castle, but the village churches seem to epitomise the rare beauty of Sussex, which is essentially intimate.

Literary associations

West Sussex has forged links with many famous men over the years – among them the French-born writer, poet and politician Hilaire Belloc (1870–1953), who lived at Shipley, south of Horsham, for many years and explored much of his beloved Sussex on foot. Most famously, he walked across the county, starting at Robertsbridge in East Sussex and finishing at South Harting on the border between West Sussex and Hampshire, covering a distance of some 90 miles. That was in 1902, at a time when Belloc feared that what he loved most in the world might soon fade and die. He was right to be fearful. A way of life so familiar to Belloc and his generation was beginning to crumble and soon the brutal effects of the Great War would be felt even in this quintessentially English corner of the country.

The effects of this great social upheaval would last for decades and West Sussex would never be the same again. Even today, the county – and the country at large – remain in a constant state of flux. But there are aspects of the West Sussex countryside that remain reassuringly timeless and permanent and many of the walks in this guide reflect life's constant cycle and predictable pattern. The seasons come and go – offering the walker something different yet familiar each time he sets foot outside. Who could fail to be captured by the beauty and majesty of a spectacular downland

The River Arun at Littlehampton

view on a glorious summer's day or the rich golden hues of a sun-lit beech wood in autumn?

Hilaire Belloc may no longer be with us but thankfully his memory has been preserved and his spirit is all around us. He is one of a number of great writers and poets who are recalled by a new long-distance path, the West Sussex Literary Trail, which connects Horsham in the north-east corner of West Sussex with Chichester, close to its coast. The 55-mile trail is linked to many distinguished literary figures who enjoyed close associations with West Sussex. William Blake and Shelley savoured its rural landscape, Tennyson lived at Black Down near Midhurst for the last 24 years of his life, Keats was inspired by the breathtaking beauty and medieval lines of Chichester, and Oscar Wilde penned *The Importance of Being Earnest* in Worthing.

West Sussex is blessed with many other popular trails, of course. The best known among them is surely the South Downs Way, which runs like a thread for 100 miles over the ridge of the Downs and in high summer is often strewn with walkers and cyclists. The route links Eastbourne in East Sussex with Winchester and offers some of the best views and most exhilarating walking in southern England. The Sussex Border Path is less familiar but nonetheless a firm favourite with many walkers. Opened in 1980, the trail meanders for many miles along the boundary between West and East Sussex. Elsewhere, there is the attractive High Weald Landscape Trail and the wonderfully varied Monarch's Way, the latter using a little poetic licence to follow Charles II's escape route in 1651. The huge growth in the leisure industry in recent years has seen many new trails springing up across the country and West Sussex is no exception. Inevitably, some of them coincide in places but happily they never fall short of their main objective – to reflect the character and beauty of the countryside.

That, of course, is the intention of this guide. All the walks in the book recall something that is unique to West Sussex, each one bringing a different facet of the landscape. For example, two very different stately homes, a disused canal, a much-loved steam railway, a magical yew forest and a colourful racecourse are some of the more unusual features to be found acting as a fascinating backdrop to the routes. Obviously, a number of the walks explore the South Downs at close quarters, while others touch on their dramatic and very English beauty by providing tantalising views from afar. Elsewhere, there are walks beneath wide skies around the meandering boundaries of Chichester Harbour, offering scenery of a very different kind. This is one of the great natural features of Britain's beautiful coastline and though the walking is flat, there is much to see – both on the water and off. One of the walks here even has a ferry crossing thrown in for good measure. The thickly wooded, hilly country surrounding Midhurst cries out to be explored on foot and the undulating landscape of the High Weald, where the two counties meet, is also a haven for walkers.

In terms of walk distances and what to choose, it is never easy to know where to start. The advice to complete beginners is usually to begin with the shortest and easiest routes. These are straightforward and unlikely to pose a problem for the outdoor novice. The next stage would be to tackle something longer and a little more ambitious and gradually work up from there. It's really a matter of common sense and knowledge of your own personal ability. The walks are categorised in order of difficulty and physical effort and GPS (Global Positioning System) readings are included to offer additional help and reassurance. Wear sturdy walking boots and carry a rucksack with the bare essentials – especially on the longer, more adventurous walks. This should include waterproof clothing – crucial on any walk, particularly on routes over exposed downland where there is little tree cover – plenty of water, a light snack, a camera and a torch – just in case. Though this guide includes an Ordnance Survey map extract to accompany the text in each chapter, you should also include an appropriate copy of the Explorer or Landranger series. These days, most people would have a mobile telephone with them – which, of course, is very useful in case of emergency, but do not assume you will always get a signal while out walking.

They say life is full of coincidences. Within hours of the walks described in this guide being completed, the Government made a formal announcement that the South Downs of Sussex were at last to be given formal National Park status after a 60-year delay. The walking country that lies within the boundaries of the new park is key to the enjoyment of this book. But, above all, the guide's objective is to highlight the unique variety and enormous diversity of this special region of southern England and provide many hours of exercise and pleasure in the beautiful surroundings of West Sussex and the South Downs.

This book includes a list of waypoints alongside the description of the walk, so that you can enjoy the full benefits of gps should you wish to. For more information on using your gps, read the *Pathfinder® Guide GPS for Walkers,* by gps teacher and navigation trainer, Clive Thomas (ISBN 978-0-7117-4445-5). For essential information on map reading and basic navigation, read the *Pathfinder® Guide Map Reading Skills* by outdoor writer, Terry Marsh (ISBN 978-0-7117-4978-8). Both titles are available in bookshops or can be ordered online at www.totalwalking.co.uk

Durford Heath and Rogate Common

		GPS waypoints
Start	Durford Heath	☑ SU 790 259
Distance	3½ miles (5.6km)	Ⓐ SU 787 250
Height gain	425 feet (130m)	Ⓑ SU 787 239
Approximate time	2 hours	Ⓒ SU 794 240
Parking	National Trust car park, (inconspicuous entrance on the south side of the road to Rogate, close to B2070 at Hill Brow)	Ⓓ SU 799 242
		Ⓔ SU 797 248
		Ⓕ SU 793 255
Route terrain	Largely through extensive woodland following paths and tracks	
Ordnance Survey maps	Landranger 197 (Chichester & The South Downs), Explorer 133 (Haslemere & Petersfield)	

A short walk mainly through woodland that uses part of the Sussex Border Path on the northern edge of West Sussex. The return leg is mainly uphill, but there are few taxing gradients and the going is mainly over good ground (though note the warning about brambles and nettles after point Ⓑ – it would be unwise to wear shorts). Look out for birds such as green woodpeckers, goldcrests and greenfinches.

Durford's only claim to fame was its abbey, a Premonstratensian house of the 11th century situated near Rogate village. When it was dissolved in 1539, Henry VIII's commissioner found it 'The poorest abbey I have seen – far in debt and in decay'.

☑ Go through the pedestrian gate into the wood and walk down with a fence to the right past rhododendrons. Near the National Trust sign at the bottom, fork left to follow the waymarked Sussex Border Path on a sandy path that descends gently through pine trees.

The Sussex Border Path is a challenging long-distance trail that covers 152 miles between Emsworth and Rye. It more or less follows the

Weather-boarded cottage near Durford

boundary of the Saxon kingdom of Sussex, taking in parts of Hampshire, Surrey and Kent as well.

There is another track to the right that runs alongside for some distance. Keep ahead at Long Bottom, where another path crosses your route. Stay on the Border Path, which continues to descend as the track to the right veers away.

Take the right fork when the track divides **Ⓐ**. The path climbs out of conifers and there are views over rolling countryside before the path joins with a track from the right. At the bottom of a dip the track, still part of the Sussex Border Path, crosses a footpath. Keep ahead to climb the hill and pass the drive to the left that goes to Carrols.

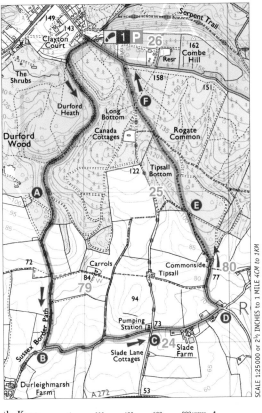

Where the track swings under trees to the right and begins to descend steeply take the sunken lane on the left **Ⓑ**. Here brambles snatch at clothing but the romantic character of bygone Sussex survives, when many roads and lanes were like this. The illusion is only slightly marred by the A272 being two fields away to the right. If horses have not used the track recently, nettles may prove to be as troublesome as the brambles. Fork right when a bridleway goes to the left to reach a lane by a pumping-station **Ⓒ**.

Keep ahead along the lane to pass Slade Farm. Continue for 80 yds past the picturesque thatched and weatherboarded cottage at Little Slade, then turn left at the next junction **Ⓓ**.

Make a short climb up the lane to Commonside. After Commonside House, keep to the bridleway, which bears left into the woods and begins a steady climb. There is a fine view to the south-west just before another bridleway joins from the left **Ⓔ**. Keep ahead into the pine trees, until the gradient eases at a half-hidden bridleway fingerpost on your left.

Fork left here, and continue through the thick undergrowth. Cross the track to Canada Cottages at a staggered junction, and continue climbing on the main signposted bridleway to the five-way junction near Long Bottom **Ⓕ**.

Keep ahead onto the major track and turn left at the road. From here it is 300 yds back to the start. ●

Kingley Vale

Start	West Stoke
Distance	3½ miles (5.6km)
Height gain	475 feet (145m)
Approximate time	2 hours
Parking	Car park ½ mile north of B2178 at East Ashling
Route terrain	Paths through historic yew forest and steep climb to open downland
Ordnance Survey maps	Landranger 197 (Chichester & The South Downs), Explorer 120 (Chichester)

GPS waypoints

✐ SU 824 088
Ⓐ SU 823 099
Ⓑ SU 819 110

Kingley Vale lies below the South Downs and its thickly wooded slopes embrace the finest yew forest in Europe, now a National Nature Reserve managed and conserved by English Nature. After a short walk across open country from the village of West Stoke to reach the edge of the vale, you follow a nature trail around it, winding through dark and eerie groves of ancient and gnarled yew trees before heading up onto the open downland of Bow Hill. From the top there are fine views across the downs towards Chichester harbour and the coast. You then descend into the wooded vale again, finally retracing your steps to the start to conclude a most fascinating walk.

The hamlet of West Stoke, lying in a quiet and remote setting near the foot of the downs, comprises little more than farm buildings, a large house and a small, simple church.

✐ Begin by going through a gate in the corner of the car park, at a public footpath sign, and walk along a track between trees and fences. There are pleasant views on both sides across tree-fringed fields, and ahead the wooded slopes of Kingley Vale below Bow Hill soon come into sight.

After ¾ mile you arrive at a gate on the edge of the nature reserve Ⓐ. Go through it and keep ahead, passing by the Field Museum to reach the start of the numbered nature trail. You now follow the trail in an anti-clockwise direction around the vale; there are 24 numbered green posts in all. The first part is particularly fascinating as you walk through groves of ancient yews – huge and gnarled trees, some of which are at least 500 years old. One legend claims that a grove was planted to commemorate a victory here against the Vikings in the 9th century. There are other trees as well, including an equally ancient and gnarled oak, and a series of information boards. Bear right on emerging from the trees.

After a while the trail climbs alongside the right-hand edge of the reserve, keeping left above the trees on the higher ground to reach the top of Bow Hill, where you meet a straight track at post 19

Ancient yews in Kingley Vale

B. To the right are two of the four Devil's Humps (the other two are hidden by trees) – Bronze Age tombs erected around 500 BC. It is worthwhile making a brief detour to them for the magnificent all-round view: westwards over the downs and eastwards to the coast and inlets of Chichester harbour.

Level with the Devil's Humps, bear left to join a parallel path which re-enters woodland and passes through another dark and eerie part of the yew forest, heading gently downhill above the rim of the steep-sided, thickly wooded vale. Keep curving gradually to the left all the while, to reach the edge of the nature reserve **A**. Turn right and retrace your steps along the track to West Stoke. ●

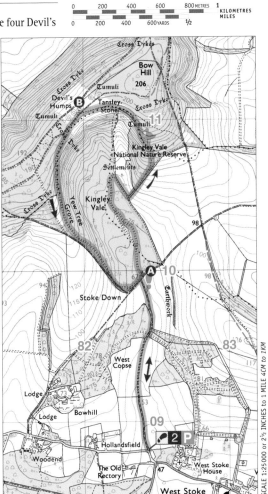

Pulborough Brooks

Start	Pulborough
Distance	3¾ miles (6km)
Height gain	180 feet (55m)
Approximate time	2 hours
Parking	Car park off Brooks Way
Route terrain	Riverside and field paths and tracks
Ordnance Survey maps	Landranger 197 (Chichester & the South Downs), Explorer 121 (Arundel & Pulborough)

GPS waypoints

- ✒ TQ 053 185
- Ⓐ TQ 053 179
- Ⓑ TQ 053 173
- Ⓒ TQ 058 167
- Ⓓ TQ 061 171
- Ⓔ TQ 060 179

Immediately to the south of Pulborough lies a fascinating patchwork of wet meadows and sprawling marshes, with impressive views of the South Downs escarpment on the horizon. Thrown in for good measure is the River Arun, which skirts this evocative landscape, and midway round there is the chance to visit an historic Sussex church and a short optional spur to the Pulborough Brooks Nature Reserve Visitor Centre.

✒ With Pulborough library behind you, make for the far end of the car park and go down the steps to reach a path by a tall brick wall. Turn left and walk down to several quaint cottages on the right immediately before a gate, stile and public footpath fingerpost. The rolling hills of the South Downs define the horizon to the south. Cross the meadows to a ditch and stream and then keep ahead with a dyke and bank on the right, still heading south towards the distant escarpment. There are pleasant views from here back to Pulborough. Make for a waymark where the walk meets another footpath. Go forward over a footbridge Ⓐ and keep ahead with the River Arun to your right. In dry conditions both the upper and lower riverside path offer pleasant, gentle walking throughout the seasons.

Cross two stiles and continue now on the upper path to the point where it veers away from the Arun riverbank Ⓑ. Follow a grassy meadow track, which sweeps left and then right to reach a gate, stile and waymark. Follow the track uphill to pass two gates – one giving access to Winpenny Hide, the other to Nettleys Hide. Disregard these turnings and mount the stile in front of you into the field. Go diagonally across the pasture to a further stile and a gate. Bear left and head down to the field corner where there is another stile Ⓒ. Cross it and continue ahead, following the path to Wiggonholt church. This historic place of worship, which has no patron saint, was built after the Norman Conquest for the use of yeoman and tenant farmers as well as shepherds and herdsman on Pulborough Brooks. The original walls are 12th or 13th-century and most of the windows are in the perpendicular style.

Leave the church via the lychgate and gate; turn left and head up the slope almost as far as a waymark and gate by a house. Turn right over the stile into pasture and follow the path to the Pulborough Brooks Nature Reserve Visitor Centre. As well as a shop, **tearoom**, terrace and children's play area, there are wetland and heathland trails to enjoy.

Situated in the glorious Arun Valley, Pulborough Brooks is acknowledged as one of Europe's major wetland sites, supporting half of the valley's breeding wading birds and more than half of its wintering water birds. There are also heathland and grassland areas, woodland, hedgerows and bushes, which are vital for many species of birds, plants and insects.

The RSPB acquired this site in 1989 at a time when few wetland birds were visiting the area. The use of traditional farming practices and the careful control of water here has resulted in the return of much of the wildlife.

Return by the same route and on reaching the stile at the top of the meadow near the house, turn left to a stile by the sign for Wiggonholt church. Cross the drive to the Old Rectory to a stile and follow the footpath as it skirts a field, keeping to the left-hand boundary. Cross a stile in the corner of the pasture and keep ahead, over to the left. Descend to the next stile and continue in the next pasture on the obvious path. Make for the corner and cross a stile. Turn right **D** along a track and at a junction with another track, turn left at the footpath sign, descending some steps to a sunken path between banks of vegetation. Negotiate

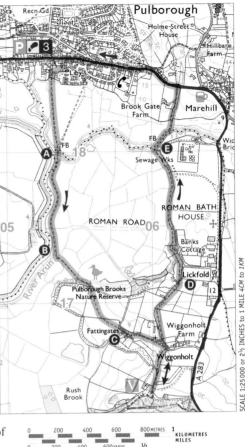

SCALE 1:25 000 or 2½ INCHES to 1 MILE 4CM to 1KM

0	200	400	600	800 METRES	1
					KILOMETRES MILES
0	200	400	600 YARDS	½	

the next stile and keep right, enjoying good views of Pulborough Brooks.

Pass alongside a cottage with a low roof and beyond the next stile continue ahead on the clear path, which soon becomes enclosed by hedging and trees. When it breaks cover once more, cross a stile and head for a footbridge **E**. On the far side keep right along the waterside path and shortly bear left to a stile and fingerpost. Follow the enclosed path towards Pulborough and emerge at the road opposite the entrance to Holme Manor. To the right along the road lies the **White Horse** pub. Turn left and follow the road back into Pulborough. On reaching its centre, turn left into Brooks Way. ●

PULBOROUGH BROOKS ● 17

Climbing Beach and the River Arun

		GPS waypoints
Start	Climping Beach	
Distance	3¾ miles (6km)	⬛ TQ 006 008
Height gain	Negligible	Ⓐ TQ 007 008
Approximate time	2 hours	Ⓑ TQ 002 013
Parking	Car park off the A259 west of Littlehampton	Ⓒ TQ 015 019 Ⓓ TQ 021 021 Ⓔ TQ 016 012
Route terrain	Level paths and tracks, some road walking, well-trodden trail along shoreline	
Ordnance Survey maps	Landranger 197 (Chichester & the South Downs), Explorer 121 (Arundel & Pulborough)	

A quick glance at a map of the coast of southern England reveals few pockets of undeveloped land. However, at Climping, between Bognor Regis and Littlehampton, there is a rare stretch of unspoilt coastline – perfect for exploring on foot. From the sea, the walk heads inland across pleasantly flat fields and golf links before hugging the windy shore on the return leg.

One of the main attractions of Climping Beach is its remote and secluded setting. If you do not know this area, the signposts might cause some confusion. Though this is Climping Beach, the actual village is some distance inland. The nearest community to the beach is Atherington. The medieval church and various dwellings now lie beneath the sea, which has gradually encroached upon the land.

🗒 From the car park make for the road Ⓐ and head inland, passing between trees and the entrance to **Bailiffscourt Hotel** on the left. Keep ahead along the road heading in a north-westerly direction to reach the **Black Horse** pub on the right. Pass it and then take the next footpath on the right, by several thatched cottages Ⓑ. Soon the track bends left . As it does so,

continue ahead across farmland to a junction with a byway. Head straight over and follow the path across the fields, making for some abandoned outbuildings.

On reaching a track on a bend, keep right and as it swings right take the waymarked path. Initially, it runs alongside a hedge. Beyond it head out across the open field, cross a concrete footbridge and bear left at the footpath sign to follow the Ryebank Rife, a deep ditch. Follow the Rife, keeping it on your left, and on reaching a footpath sign, go diagonally across the pasture to the right-hand corner of a belt of trees (if the field has recently been ploughed, follow the boundary) where there is a footpath sign and a stile. Beyond is Ferry Road Ⓒ. Turn right here and follow a straight stretch east towards

Littlehampton. Walk along to the outskirts of the town where you approach a turning on the right for Littlehampton Golf Club **D**. Before taking the turning, continue for a few paces to a footbridge spanning the River Arun. There are good views of the river both upstream and down and the town centre and railway station are a short walk from here.

The Arun, which is fast flowing, reaches up to seven knots during the spring tides. Much of the area's long history is focused on this river. Littlehampton was a thriving port during the Middle Ages, when stone from Normandy was landed here in order to construct many of the county's churches and castles. Much later it became a fashionable seaside resort with its seafront lined with attractive and imposing Victorian and Edwardian villas.

Return to the road to Littlehampton Golf Club **D** and follow it towards West Beach and the fairways. On reaching a car park sign, veer right and follow the enclosed path to a kissing-gate. Briefly cross the golf course and return to the enclosed path, following it through woodland. The greens and fairways can be seen as you cut between the trees.

At intervals, between gaps in the woodland, there are striking views towards the coast and in the direction of Littlehampton. Continue on the path and at length you approach a house – The Mill. Disregard the path on the right here and keep left **E**. Keep going on the footpath and before long it emerges from the trees at West Beach. Almost immediately an interpretation board is seen, explaining how the effects of the elements have influenced stretches of Sussex coastline over the centuries.

This lonely coast is noted for its shingle banks, which support vegetation here and there, as well as its fragile but active sand dunes. Only six sites survive on the south coast between Kent and Cornwall and three of them are on this stretch. Not surprisingly, the National Trust protects several miles of coastline here.

Follow the footpath sign towards Climping, keeping to the edge of the beach with the sea away to your left. At length you pass a byway and then return to the car park where the walk began.

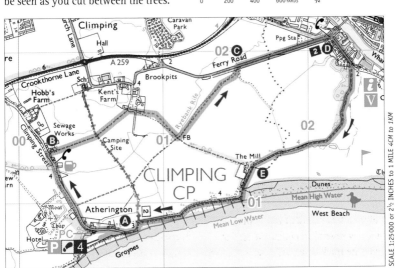

Three Commons Walk

		GPS waypoints
Start	Iping Common	SU 852 220
Distance	4 miles (6.4km)	**A** SU 846 215
Height gain	330 feet (100m)	**B** SU 842 217
Approximate time	2 hours	**C** SU 841 227
Parking	Car park on west side of Iping to	**D** SU 853 228
	Elsted road, south of A272 at	**E** SU 856 221
	Stedham	
Route terrain	Common land, open heath, farmland and woodland	
Ordnance Survey maps	Landranger 197 (Chichester & The South Downs), Explorer 133 (Haslemere & Petersfield)	

The sandy commons in the north-west corner of the county provide a habitat for a wide range of birds, plants and insects and are excellent for walking. This route covers three of these commons (Iping, Trotton and Stedham) and, by way of contrast, returns close to the River Rother via the lovely village of Stedham.

Take the bridleway that passes through the car park, leaving it between wooden posts to reach a barrier. Keep ahead, ignoring a Heathland Trail on the left. Heather covers the sandy

ground to the left and there is woodland on the right. Nightjars and Dartford warblers are two uncommon species of birds who find this blend of woodland and heath an excellent habitat, which also suits the silver-studded blue butterfly.

Branch right at a sign for the Serpent

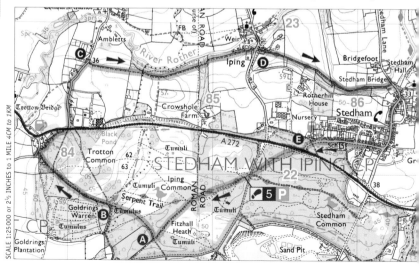

SCALE 1:25 000 or 2½ INCHES to 1 MILE 4CM to 1KM

| 0 | 200 | 400 | 600 | 800 METRES | 1 |
| 0 | 200 | 400 | 600 YARDS | ½ | KILOMETRES MILES |

Iping Common

Trail. Keep to the path alongside light woodland. When this emerges from the trees into a grassy area covered with bracken and dotted with silver birch trees, avoid a bridleway on the right and branch half left at the next Serpent Trail sign. The sand underfoot is dazzling, and there are pine trees by the bridleway that give a fragrant scent of resin on a hot day.

The bridleway meets another one in a stand of pines **Ⓐ**. Turn right at the bridleway arrow (in wet weather you may have to detour slightly to keep dry feet). The bridleway crosses another track before climbing over a stretch of heath to reach a waymark and junction by some trees **Ⓑ**. Keep right here, avoid a turning on the right and continue ahead. Later descend on a sunken bridleway, following the path alongside Lovehill Cottage. On reaching the road, the walk continues to the right via a footpath. To visit the **Keepers Arms,** keep ahead along the lane for a short distance.

Climb a slope with a garden to the left and turn left at the top to join a track. Keep ahead on it to reach the A272. Cross the main road to the lane opposite, signposted to Chithurst. This is a village with a monastery, so do not be surprised to see cowled figures in the neighbourhood.

Walk up the lane to reach a row of cottages where the lane bends left. Turn right **Ⓒ** onto a footpath that crosses the ditch by a plank bridge and then follows the edge of a field. Continue to follow the obvious path until eventually it enters woodland where you may spot deer. Cross a footbridge and keep going through the trees until the path swings left to come to a gate on the right. Go through this and along another stretch of field-edge path. Iping village is to the left when you reach a lane, but the walk continues on the bridleway opposite that is cobbled as it climbs from the lane. It joins a drive by Coachman's Cottage.

After 50 yds leave the drive to the right **Ⓓ**, going through an iron gate and past a luxuriant growth of bamboos. A little farther on there is a glimpse of the River Rother, flowing below to the left. The path descends steadily to Stedham Bridge – pause on the bridge to enjoy the view of the hall and read the notice warning drivers not to leave their locomotives standing on the structure (presumably it would be a convenient place to take on water).

Return from the bridge to walk through Stedham. Turn right at the village sign and pass the school and the **Hamilton Arms**. Go right **Ⓔ** at the main road and as you approach a road junction sign in the opposite verge, cross over to a gap in the undergrowth. A gate takes the bridleway into woodland and then across the heath. Pass gates on the right and then exit to the road. Cross over and return to the car park. ●

St Leonard's Forest

		GPS waypoints
Start	Roosthole car park 1 mile north of Mannings Heath	✔ TQ 208 297
Distance	4 miles (6.4km)	Ⓐ TQ 210 295
Height gain	375 feet (115m)	Ⓑ TQ 207 292
		Ⓒ TQ 202 298
Approximate time	2 hours	Ⓓ TQ 201 307
Parking	Forestry Commission car park	Ⓔ TQ 216 311
Route terrain	Mainly woodland paths and tracks with some open stretches	Ⓕ TQ 217 302
Ordnance Survey maps	Landranger 187 (Dorking & Reigate), Explorer 134 (Crawley & Horsham)	

St Leonard's Forest lies between Horsham and Crawley and in the Middle Ages was one of a series of adjacent, thickly wooded areas that occupied the 'Forest Ridge' of the Sussex Weald. Nowadays it is a pleasant mixture of conifer and broad-leaved woodland, farmland and heathland, which are all included in this easy walk, as is one of the ubiquitous hammer ponds, a reflection of the past importance of the iron industry in this area.

In the early 19th century William Cobbett described St Leonard's Forest as a 'miserable tract of heath and fern and bushes and sand'. It was the demand for charcoal from the local ironmasters that led to the felling of much of the forest, especially during the 16th and 17th centuries at the height of the Wealden iron industry, but some traditional woodland survives, considerably augmented by the more recent conifer plantations of the Forestry Commission. The forest is thought to get its name from a former chapel within it, dedicated to St Leonard.

🥾 From the car park head back to the road and turn left along it for ¼ mile and turn down the first lane on the right Ⓐ, signposted to Mannings Heath. The lane heads gently downhill. At a left-hand bend turn right over a stile Ⓑ, at a public footpath sign, to follow a path across a field, soon curving left to keep alongside a wire fence on the right to another stile. Climb it, entering the woodlands of Alder Copse, and keep along the inside

Roosthole Pond in St Leonard's Forest

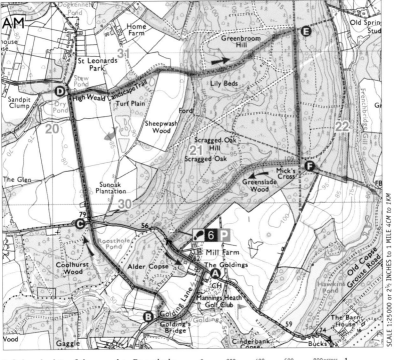

left-hand edge of the wood to Roosthole
Pond. This is one of the numerous
hammer ponds in the forest; the overflow
from them provided the power for the
hammers used in the iron industry.

Cross the end of the pond, continue
gently uphill, now along the inside right-
hand edge of Coolhurst Wood, and rejoin
the road **C**. Cross over and walk along
the broad, straight, tree-lined track
opposite. After ¹/₂ mile you reach a metal
gate; just in front of it turn right **D**, at a
footpath sign, onto a narrow path that
squeezes between trees and bushes on the
left and a hedge and wire fence bordering
a field on the right. This path may be
overgrown and awkward in places. When
you reach the end of the field bear left
along an obvious and easier path across
an area of rough grass and scrub, cross a
track, then climb a stile and continue
across an open landscape of grassland
fringed by trees.

Follow the track as it sweeps right,
making for a wire fence at the field edge

and keep alongside it to descend into
woodland. Keep ahead at a public footpath sign and path junction. Pass to the
right of a shallow pond and continue
gently uphill along a broad path through
mixed woodland. Keep a sharp look-out
for a public footpath sign (and a sign for
the High Weald Landscape Trail) by a
slight right-hand bend which directs you
to bear left along a narrow path, still
heading gently uphill. At a public footpath
sign cross a track and continue across an
area of heathland, past another public
footpath sign and continuing to the next
one at a crossing of tracks and paths **E**.

Turn right here to walk along a wide,
geometrically straight track and after
¹/₂ mile you reach a public footpath sign at
another crossing of tracks and paths. Keep
ahead for a few yards and then turn right
F along an attractive forest track which
leads directly back to the car park. ●

Devil's Dyke

		GPS waypoints
Start	Devil's Dyke Hotel	🖉 TQ 258 110
Distance	3¾ miles (6km)	Ⓐ TQ 264 113
Height gain	655 feet (200m)	Ⓑ TQ 260 119
Approximate time	2½ hours	Ⓒ TQ 258 123
Parking	Car park adjoining hotel (National Trust)	Ⓓ TQ 250 124
		Ⓔ TQ 250 125
Route terrain	Downland, woodland and farmland paths and tracks	Ⓕ TQ 246 113
		Ⓖ TQ 253 107
Ordnance Survey maps	Landranger 198 (Brighton & Lewes), Explorer 122 (Brighton & Hove)	

Starting from one of southern England's finest viewpoints, the rest of this walk continues in the same vein. The climb back to the ridge at the end is an exhilarating finale to a route which combines the best features of downland—and field walking, as well as visiting two charming villages.

On a fine day you may have to arrive early to find a place in the car park at the Devil's Dyke Hotel. The spectacular view

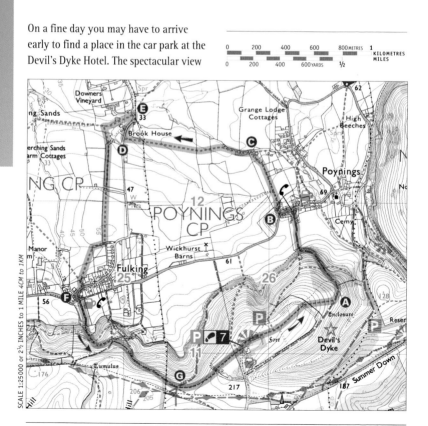

makes this a popular venue, and its airiness attracts kite flyers.

The fine panorama from Devil's Dyke

With your back to the hotel, turn right and walk past the large stone memorial seat (which dates from 1928 when the Dyke estate was given to the nation), continuing in a north-easterly direction along the crest of the ridge. Parallel paths lead to two stiles just a few paces apart. Take the right-hand stile and descend to another path below **A** which follows a ledge. Turn left onto this bridleway and follow it northwards to a beautiful wood, where it begins to descend more steeply and can become very muddy after wet weather. Keep right at the National Trust sign for Devil's Dyke. The subsequent level path into Poynings can also be muddy. When this path reaches the main street, turn right if you wish to visit the **Royal Oak**, otherwise turn left. On the apex of the following bend look for a footpath sign on the left that points into a short lane on the right **B**. This leads to a gate, which opens into a long meadow. Go ahead on a path and at the far end of the meadow go through a gate to join a track.

Turn left to a stile **C** and follow an attractive path running along the bank of a stream. Cross the stream by a bridge and then make for another stile on the far side of the meadow. Cross the next field on a sunken path to reach a stile. Cross the small field that follows to reach a lane **D**.

Turn right and follow the lane for 250 yds before turning left immediately after a small bridge **E** onto a concrete drive signposted 'Brookside'. Bear left immediately onto a path running along-side trees by a stream to find a bridge over it on the left. Cross this and follow a field path heading south. Bear left initially towards loose boxes and make for two stiles in the right-hand corner of the field. Keep ahead along the field edge, cross two stiles to a farm track and continue ahead. Make for the field corner near houses, cross a stile and bear right to a kissing-gate.

Take the left edge of the field for about 75 yds, then bear diagonally left across an arable field, making for the right-hand end of a brick wall largely hidden by vegetation. Climb a few steps to a kissing-gate, then follow the left edge of a small paddock to reach the road through Fulking.

Turn right down the lane, and directly before the **Shepherd & Dog** there is a bridleway on the left **F**. Take this and after 50 yds look for steps up the bank on the right, from which a footpath leads off. This footpath provides walkers with a taxing climb up the Fulking escarpment before open downland is reached. Keep straight on at a junction of paths **G**, where the **Devil's Dyke Hotel** comes into view.

Loxwood and the Wey South Path

Start	Loxwood	GPS waypoints	
Distance	4½ miles (7.2km)	✐ TQ 042 311	
Height gain	150 feet (45m)	Ⓐ TQ 041 314	
		Ⓑ TQ 040 319	
Approximate time	2 hours	Ⓒ TQ 043 331	
Parking	Visitor car park by the Onslow Arms	Ⓓ TQ 028 324	
Route terrain	Level field paths and tracks, disused canal towpath		
Ordnance Survey maps	Landranger 186 (Aldershot & Guildford), Explorer 134 (Crawley & Horsham)		

This easy, level walk perfectly illustrates the story of a bold attempt to link London with the Sussex coast via our complex inland waterway system. Beginning by the old Wey & Arun Canal at Loxwood, the walk encounters a patchwork of fields and meadows before coinciding with a section of the Sussex Border Path. The last lap follows the route of the canal, in places derelict and abandoned, elsewhere expertly restored and renewed.

✐ From the visitor car park adjacent to the **Onslow Arms**, follow the towpath to the road (B2133), turn right and cross the canal. Follow the road through the village to the next footpath

The Onslow Arms

on the right. Take this tarmac path and cut between hedges to reach Loxwood Surgery. Keep going through a housing estate and then turn right at the T-junction. Pass Burley Close Ⓐ and turn left shortly afterwards into the intriguingly named Spy Lane. Follow the road between houses and bungalows and pass the Emmanuel Fellowship Chapel on the right-hand side.

Turn right Ⓑ at a stile immediately after the chapel to skirt the Emmanuel Fellowship playing field. Follow the path to the next stile and cut through a belt of woodland. Emerging from the trees, head for the right-hand perimeter of the field, aiming for a stile in the corner. Clamber over it; turn immediately left to a fingerpost and further stile. Cross over and keep ahead across farmland, at length passing alongside Songhurst New Farm. Follow the path along to the field corner and make for a stile just to the right of a galvanised gate. Join a single-track lane and follow it in a northerly direction, passing a house on the right. Away to the left across the fields is Mallards Farm.

Continue on the farm lane as it cuts through a rural patchwork of fields and hedgerows. On reaching a junction with the Sussex Border Path **C**, turn left and pass Songhurst House. Keep going to the road, reaching it opposite the **Sir Roger Tichborne** pub. Turn left and follow it for a short distance, as far as Oakhurst Lane on the right. Take the turning and follow the lane up a gentle slope to Oakhurst Farm. Pass alongside timber barns and go straight ahead on

the Sussex Border Path when the track bends right. Skirt a field to reach trees, cross a bridleway and continue through a belt of woodland. Pass a footpath on the left and continue on the Sussex Border Path for about 100 yds to a junction **D**. Turn left and follow the Wey South Path beside the disused canal.

The Wey & Arun Canal is a fascinating example of the skill and ingenuity of the men who built our splendid 3,000-mile inland waterway system. Especially when you consider the idea behind this 23-mile canal was a good deal more complicated than it might appear on the surface, presenting the designers and builders with many

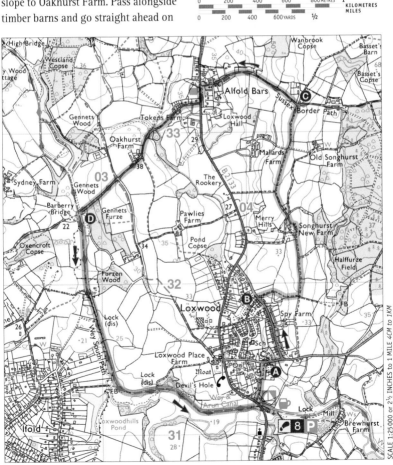

The Wey & Arun Canal at Loxwood

headaches and challenges along the way. It was constructed in 1816 to connect the Wey and Arun rivers and therefore form the last link in a chain that represented a continuous waterway between London and the south coast at Littlehampton.

In its day, the canal carried a varied assortment of cargo – including countless barge loads of bullion from Portsmouth to the Bank of England in London, guarded by Redcoats. For a while the Wey & Arun was a great success but in time it fell into decline – like many other inland waterways around the country that were once the proud achievements of pioneering engineers and now lay forgotten and abandoned. It was the growing success of the new railway age that saw off what became known as 'London's lost route to the sea' and the Wey & Arun Canal finally closed in 1871.

However, 100 years after the canal ceased to be operational, a group of dedicated and enthusiastic canal supporters established what became known as the Wey & Arun Canal Trust. Their aim was to restore the canal as a public amenity and revive its varied range of wildlife habitats. Since 1970, 11 locks, 24 bridges and two aqueducts have been restored or rebuilt. Much work has been done and in places the canal is a thriving waterway once more, but there is much still to be done and funding is always a vital issue. The Trust's members know that the restoration programme will continue for many years to come.

Go through two gates and pass a bridleway on the right with houses visible here. Look for a Wey & Arun Canal stone donated by Ted, Jeanne and Toby Williams in 1999 and keep going on the old towpath to pass alongside wooden panel fencing. Avoid a footpath on the right before passing beneath telegraph lines. Continue to a bridge where a footpath crosses the former canal and keep ahead on the Wey South Path, following the track back to Loxwood. Pass under the road by the Onslow Arms and return to the car park. ●

Horsted Keynes and the Bluebell Railway

		GPS waypoints
Start	Horsted Keynes station	✎ TQ 371 292
Distance	5 miles (8km)	Ⓐ TQ 373 296
Height gain	475 feet (145m)	Ⓑ TQ 375 308
Approximate time	2½ hours	Ⓒ TQ 384 306
Parking	At start	Ⓓ TQ 383 284
Route terrain	Field and woodland paths and tracks	
Ordnance Survey maps	Landranger 198 (Brighton & Lewes), Explorer 135 (Ashdown Forest)	

The authentically preserved railway station at Horsted Keynes is one of the more unusual features on this delightfully varied walk, capturing the flavour of train travel as it used to be in the great days of steam. From the station the walk skirts the track to join the Sussex Border Path en route to delightful Broadhurst Lake and Horsted Keynes Church of St Giles. There is an optional spur to the village centre.

The famous Bluebell Railway recalls the heyday of the railway era, and the station at Horsted Keynes, which lies on that line, is both that and a very

Steam trains at Horsted Keynes

effective museum dedicated to the golden age of steam travel. The railway, which dates back to the early 1880s, was operational until 1958 when it became one of scores of rural lines to be closed down. However, it was not out of action for long. Soon pressure was mounting to transform the former line into a major tourist attraction. By the early 1960s it was in private ownership and once again the old workhorses chugged through the Sussex countryside, complete with clouds of steam and the familiar and evocative sound of the engine's whistle.

✎ From the car park close to the station buildings, walk away from the main entrance, keeping the Bluebell Railway on your left. Pass a footpath sign and cross the footbridge, turning right on the far side of the track. Keep

Broadhurst Lake

to the path as it briefly heads away to the west to cross two stiles before returning to the railway line at a further stile **A**.

Turn left and follow the path parallel to the line to a footpath sign. Cross the track at this point to another stile and keep the railway on your left on the next stage of the walk. Cross two stiles with a single-track lane in between, and keep alongside the right-hand boundary hedge. Cross another stile and keep ahead to a kissing-gate. Follow the path across farmland to the next stile and continue by some holly trees to a footpath sign. Turn right here to the road **B**. Swing left here for about 60 yds to a stile on the right and join the route of the Sussex Border Path. Follow the path down the field and into woodland, skirting a pond and stream. Turn left on the far side of the water and head uphill between the trees to a pasture.

Turn left and follow the field edge path round to the right in the corner and down to a gap among the trees and bushes. Descend some steps beneath the branches to a footbridge and then go up the steep slope to a field. Turn left and

skirt the pasture to a gate. At the road **C** turn right and walk along to the junction with Broadhurst Manor Road. Turn left and follow it to the Sussex Border Path waymark. Turn right here and follow the drive to the entrance to historic Broadhurst Manor, now an animal sanctuary. Keep right at the gates, staying on the waymarked trail, and follow it to Broadhurst Lake, an idyllic spot on the walk. Continue on the track into Church Lane and pass the Church of St Giles on the left.

Inside the churchyard, to the right, are the graves of the former Tory Prime Minister Harold Macmillan, his wife Dorothy and their son Maurice. The Macmillans lived nearby. Born in London in 1894, Harold Macmillan joined the Grenadier Guards during the First World War and was seriously wounded. He later worked for the family publishing business but maintained his interest in politics. He became Conservative MP for Stockton-on-Tees in 1924 and was a familiar figure on the back benches until 1940 when Churchill appointed him Parliamentary Secretary to the Ministry of Supply. Defeated in the landslide victory of 1945, he later returned to politics as MP for Bromley, a position

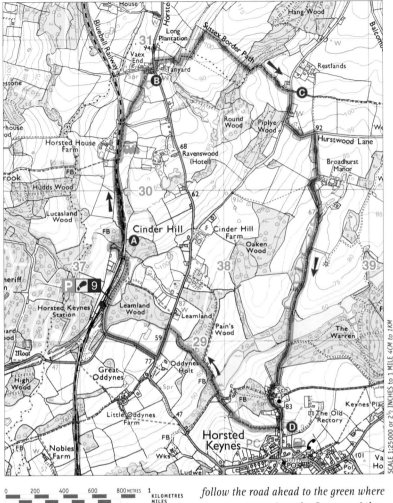

he held until his retirement in 1964. During his long career in politics, Macmillan was appointed Minister of Defence and Chancellor of the Exchequer, among other posts. He famously told the British people they'd 'never had it so good' – a phrase that is still quoted and remembered today. He was Prime Minister between 1959 and 1963 and died in 1986.

On reaching a path by a tile-hung cottage known as Timbers **D** you have a choice.

To visit the village of Horsted Keynes, *follow the road ahead to the green where* *there are two pubs – **the Crown** and **the** **Green Man**. Otherwise, take the footpath* *by Timbers and go through several gates* *to follow a fenced path into the trees.* Go through a kissing-gate, cross a track and keep ahead on the footpath. Go straight on at the next track, pass a lake and then veer left at the next fork. Turn left across a footbridge at the next footpath sign, disregard a turning on the right and clamber over two stiles to reach the road. Turn left and then take the first turning on the right (Station Approach), veering right for the Bluebell Railway and the car park where the walk began.

●

Ardingly Reservoir

		GPS waypoints
Start	Ardingly Reservoir car park	✎ TQ 335 287
Distance	5 miles (8km)	**A** TQ 335 290
Height gain	490 feet (150m)	**B** TQ 340 298
Approximate time	2½ hours	**C** TQ 340 304
Parking	At start; the car park is locked at 18.00 in summer, earlier in other months	**D** TQ 339 308
		E TQ 325 303
		F TQ 333 297
Route terrain	Woodland, parkland and lakeside paths	
Ordnance Survey maps	Landranger 187 (Dorking & Reigate) and 198 (Brighton & Lewes), Explorer 135 (Ashdown Forest)	

Ardingly (pronounced 'Arding-lye') Reservoir was constructed in 1978 and its 6 mile perimeter embraces 198 acres. The walk follows the quiet shoreline on the north side of the reservoir and also goes through Tilgate Wood, where a long footbridge spans its major arm. It is possible to lengthen the walk with a visit to Loder Valley Nature Reserve (see details below).

✎ Bear right across the foot of the dam from the information panels, climbing gently to the kissing-gate at the start of the Kingfisher Trail. Continue for 200 yds to a stile on the right **A**.

Turn right over the stile. The path begins by following the hedge on your right, then climbs across an open field to the signposted crossways at Townhouse Farm; look back here for a fine view of the reservoir and the Ouse Valley railway viaduct. Bear slightly right along a farm track, and keep ahead onto the tarred lane at Hunter's Gate. Pass Ardingly's lovely church with its ancient yew tree, turn right at the junction, and continue for a few paces more.

Turn left onto the short footpath **B** opposite Jordan's Cottage; then, at the wicket gate, turn left onto the drive that skirts the perimeter of the agricultural showground. After about ½ mile this

swings to the right **C**, and you can follow it in this direction to the **Gardeners' Arms** pub which stands close to the Royal Botanic Gardens at Wakehurst Place. One wing of the house, built by Sir Edward Culpeper in 1590, is incorporated into the existing mansion. In 1963 it became a National Trust property and was subsequently leased to the Royal Botanic Garden and acquired its nickname 'Kew in the country'.

Otherwise, fork left here through a metal gate into the woodland and follow the path to a T-junction **D**.

Turn left onto a farm drive that descends past a duckpond before the right of way bypasses Tillinghurst farmyard. After a stile by a metal gate, keep the trees to the right and drop down through the meadows. Continue past another stile and metal gate to clumps of laurels in the bottom right-hand corner. Continue down to a stile and gate and farther down pass a footpath sign and a stone in memory of Elizabeth Champion. Keep ahead with the deer fence and picnic area on the right to reach a stile. Cross over and turn left, following the woodland track as it bears right at a gate into the Loder Valley Nature Reserve and onto the long wooden footbridge over the northern arm of the reservoir. (Fifty permits each day are available in advance from the office at Wakehurst Place [tel. 01444 894066] for those wishing to explore the secret paths through Bushy Wood, or, on the far side of the bridge, Tilgate Wood. No dogs are allowed.)

Bear right after the bridge to begin climbing the steeply wooded slopes to a lane. Turn left to lose the height that you have just gained (though in compensation the lane is hardly less beautiful than the previous path), and turn right at a T-junction towards Balcombe.

Turn left through the metal gate **E** opposite Edmond's Farm onto a bridleway that follows close to the hedge to the right (do not be tempted by the field track). The bridleway descends a coomb into a narrow meadow that has trees on each side and a stream in the middle. Head for the bottom right corner to a gate, turn left through a wicket gate and follow the bridleway along the shoreline as far as the causeway. Now turn right along the roadside path for 220 yds.

Turn right through the kissing-gate **F** to rejoin the shoreline path, and follow it all the way back to the car park at the foot of the dam. ●

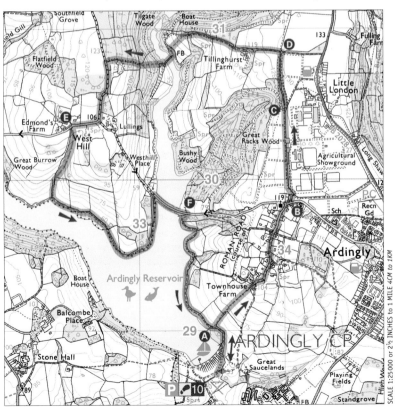

The Chidham Peninsula

		GPS waypoints
Start	Chidham	🥾 SU 793 034
Distance	5 miles (8km)	**Ⓐ** SU 796 034
Height gain	Negligible	**Ⓑ** SU 788 020
Approximate time	2½ hours	**Ⓒ** SU 780 046
Parking	Cobnor Farm amenity car park at south end of village	**Ⓓ** SU 787 044
Route terrain	Level waterside and field paths	
Ordnance Survey maps	Landranger 197 (Chichester & The South Downs), Explorer 120 (Chichester)	

Chidham faces Bosham across one of the innumerable creeks of Chichester harbour. The footpath that follows the shore of the peninsula takes the walker through a watery landscape whose loneliness is enjoyed by a variety of mud-loving seabirds: curlew, dunlin and redshank in winter and terns, oystercatchers and redshanks in summer. Sections of the walk may be difficult at times of exceptionally high tide.

🥾 Take the path from the car park that heads eastwards towards the shore, following the edge of a field. There's a lovely view of Bosham and its church ahead on the left as you walk towards the flood bank.

Ⓐ Turn right at the fingerpost and walk along the flood bank towards Cobnor Point; herons often fish the lagoons on the landward side of this path. Keep left at the next fingerpost, continuing along the flood bank until you reach the jetty where the path leaves the shore to skirt the Cobnor House Activity Centre. The path is surfaced for wheelchairs when it regains the shore.

There are good views across the channel to West Itchenor as the path turns westwards to round Cobnor Point. It leaves the low cliff for the beach soon afterwards and comes to a mud spit with the remains of old piling **Ⓑ**. The spit is an important nesting-site for seabirds (notably three species of tern), and the piling was put here in the 19th century when an attempt was made to reclaim a wide tract of land from the sea. Before that there was a tidal mill here.

Stunted oak trees stand below a low cliff and along this stretch there is a choice of paths. Follow the foreshore or

Cobnor Point

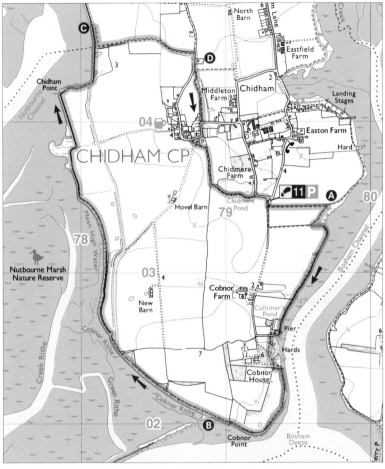

take the parallel sea wall path. Farther along it is easier to follow the latter. Thorney Island lies across the water, its ancient church standing among military installations that have become redundant. Similarly, the concrete sea defences along this part of the Chidham Peninsula seem a waste of effort, uprooted and shattered by the power of the sea.

Prinsted church can be seen ahead as the right of way approaches Chidham Point. Continue along the path, then descend the bank by steps **C** and head back below it for 100 yds before turning left to follow a hedge. Turn right when you reach the lane and walk past the large cream-painted Chedeham House **D**.

Keep straight on here to visit

*Chidham's unusually named 17th-century inn, the '***Old House at Home***'.* Otherwise turn left immediately after the house at a footpath sign and, 50 yds farther on, keep ahead at the three-way junction. Go straight on when you rejoin the lane; then, just after the tiny church with its whitewashed porch, turn left onto a lovely grassy footpath that winds past Chidmere Pond. Follow the grassy path, bear left by a telegraph pole and descend a bank to a lane. Turn right and walk for another 100 yds back to the car park.

●

Cuckfield and Ansty

		GPS waypoints
Start	Cuckfield	
Distance	5¼ miles (8.4km)	✎ TQ 304 246
Height gain	540 feet (165m)	Ⓐ TQ 303 243
Approximate time	2½ hours	Ⓑ TQ 313 239
Parking	Car park off Broad Street	Ⓒ TQ 301 233
Route terrain	Undulating paths and tracks across country to Cuckfield Park. Several short, steep climbs	Ⓓ TQ 291 233
		Ⓔ TQ 289 247
Ordnance Survey maps	Landranger 198 (Brighton & Lewes), Explorers 134 (Crawley & Horsham) and 135 (Ashdown Forest)	

One of the county's prettiest villages and the starting point for this attractive walk, Cuckfield – pronounced Cookfield – offers an impressive array of architectural styles. South of the A272, the walk follows leafy Copyhold Lane before crossing peaceful farmland to the village of Ansty, the halfway point. The final surprise is a very pleasant stroll through Cuckfield Park, with teasing glimpses of the village's tall church spire in the distance.

Cuckfield harks back to an era when powerful landowning families shaped the future of their local community, deciding what was in its best interests and making unilateral decisions for the good of the people – or so they claimed. It was thanks to the local Sargison family that Cuckfield did not end up being just another Sussex commuter town. They refused to allow the railway to run across their land so trains never came to Cuckfield. However, it has not done badly as a result and today it still retains its olde world charm and welcoming atmosphere, making it a popular tourist destination and a convenient base for London and the south coast.

After the Norman Conquest, Cuckfield was held by the Earls Warenne and granted a charter in the mid-13th century. The name means

'cuckoo-field' and a book of poetry about the village bears the delightful title *The Clearing where the Cuckoo Came.*

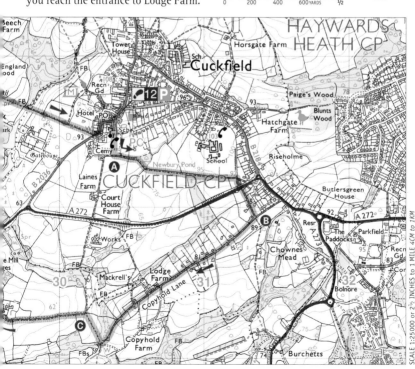 Leave the car park by taking the exit to the left of the public conveniences. At the road turn left and walk down to Church Street. Head for the lychgate by the parish church and then enter the rather large churchyard. Make for a kissing-gate **A** on the far side of the graves, turn left and follow the track. Pass a pond and climb a stile to the right of a galvanised gate. Hug the field boundary before reaching the next stile, and then follow an enclosed path cutting between clumps of holly trees. Continue on the path until you arrive at a path on the right. Follow it down to the A272 and cross it with care to a stile. Follow a delightfully shaded path through trees and on to Copyhold Lane **B**.

Turn right here and pass rows of houses. Stay on the lane and eventually you reach the entrance to Lodge Farm.

Keep ahead and when the lane bends left, head straight on at the bridleway sign, avoiding the path on the right by Copyhold Cottage. Follow the woodland path down to a tarmac drive, go straight on to cross a stream and then turn right at a footpath, almost immediately crossing a footbridge. On reaching a field, keep to the right-hand boundary and head for the corner **C**. Avoid the stile here and swing left, following the field boundary. Cross into the next field and continue all the way to the gap in the right-hand corner beyond which is a track. Follow it to the A272 at Ansty **D**.

Cross over by the **Ansty Cross** pub and take Bolney Road, turning right into Deaks Lane by St John's Church. Follow the lane along to Ansty Farm and then out of the village and into an undulating rural landscape. Stay on Deaks Lane for more than a mile and

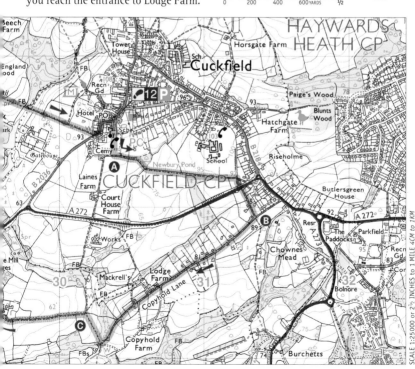

Period houses in Cuckfield

but once again it is in private ownership. With its undulating paths, clumps of trees and familiar hammer-ponds, the park is a delight and remains a popular haunt of local residents.

Follow the path ahead, cutting between trees and margins of bracken before descending to a footbridge. Climb a steep bank to a wrought-iron kissing-gate and follow the fence. Keep ahead to another kissing-gate and make for Cuckfield's distinctive church spire. The church was originally a chapel but was substantially restored in the middle of the 19th century. Inside the church are various war memorials and brasses and a very unusual ceiling with moulded bosses and a 15th century framework. This feature is linked to John of Gaunt's grandson who lived in the village in the 1460s and is understood to have gifted it to the church.

eventually turn right opposite a house called The Wylies. Go through a gate and follow the High Weald Landscape Trail down the pasture to a stile and footbridge **E**. Climb steeply through woodland to merge with another path. Keep right and walk along to the fence corner by a gate. Continue ahead, joining up with a grassy track to reach a stile and galvanised gate. The walk now passes through Cuckfield Park.

Established by an ironmaster during the reign of Elizabeth I, Cuckfield Park was the family seat of the Sargison family for several hundred years. In more recent times it became a school

Outside is a memorial to the men of the Second Battalion Post Office Rifles who were billeted and trained in Cuckfield in the early months of the First World War. They later departed for France but never returned. On reaching South Street in the village, turn left and return to the car park. ●

Wolstonbury from Hurstpierpoint

		GPS waypoints
Start	Hurstpierpoint	TQ 281 165
Distance	5¾ miles (9.2km)	**Ⓐ** TQ 276 164
Height gain	670 feet (205m)	**Ⓑ** TQ 271 156
Approximate time	3 hours	**Ⓒ** TQ 277 143
Parking	Car park off Trinity Road to the north of the village centre	**Ⓓ** TQ 284 135
		Ⓔ TQ 290 139
Route terrain	Farmland tracks and paths and one prolonged climb	**Ⓕ** TQ 288 146
		Ⓖ TQ 284 150
Ordnance Survey maps	Landranger 198 (Brighton & Lewes), Explorer 122 (Brighton & Hove)	**Ⓗ** TQ 283 156

Wolstonbury Hill, capped by an oval-shaped Iron Age fort, is one of the best viewpoints of the South Downs, so choose a clear day for the walk. The route passes through fields and meadows on the way to Wolstonbury, and there is quite a climb to the 676 feet summit. The return goes past Danny, a manor house dating from c. 1580.

Hurstpierpoint is a quiet village just off the London to Brighton road with many attractive Georgian and early-Victorian houses. The church dates from 1843 and was built to plans by Sir Charles Barry, famous for his designs of the Houses of Parliament.

🖉 From the car park take the path to the High Street, turn right and at the crossroads take the Brighton road (B2117) southwards from the village centre – the church and war memorial are to the right. After 150 yds, by the speed limit sign, take the bridleway to the right. At a crossways, go through the kissing-gate ahead and walk along the field edge to its midway point **Ⓐ**.

Bear left to cross the field to a solitary oak tree with a kissing-gate close by. Cross the next field diagonally and then turn left by a fringe of trees and reach a footbridge at the top corner of a long meadow. Turn right to join a farm track heading towards Wanbarrow Farm (and the noise of traffic) and then left onto a concrete drive.

Keep ahead to the footpath junction 200 yds beyond the farm **Ⓑ**.

Turn left, then keep ahead when the chalky track turns to the right. Continue across two fields to the B2117, cross the road, and walk up Bedlam Street for 100 yds. Follow the tarmac drive as it turns to the right, and carry on past Randolph's Farm with its high brick chimneys, keeping the converted outbuildings to the left. Now follow the track through a gate and continue into woodland in the shadow of Wolstonbury Hill.

Pass Foxhole Cottages and after 100 yds leave the drive to the left **Ⓒ** onto a field-edge bridleway. When this reaches trees the climbing begins. Cross the bridleway at the top of the woodland onto National Trust land. About 100 yds after a National Trust sign, keep right at the fork and climb the hill on the obvious path. The summit of Wolstonbury Hill is to the left on the skyline. Keep to the path around the flank of the hill and at length Jack and Jill Windmills at Clayton edge come into view. As they do, turn sharp left off the main path **D**. Head round the eastern flank of the hill now until a path is seen running downhill to the right. Take it. A stile soon comes into view below. Go over it and keep a dell to the right as you descend to a gate giving onto a bridleway **E** at the bottom of the field. Bear left onto this and then fork right on a footpath at a cottage, called The

Warenne, and follow its drive to a lane.

Turn left along the lane and follow it around the right-hand bend as far as the Victorian letterbox beside the drive to Little Danny stables **F**. (The name derives from the Saxon *danegithe*, meaning 'a haven in a valley.')

Turn left here onto the signposted footpath, crossing a plank bridge and stile into a meadow. The footpath across the meadow gives a good view of the south and east fronts of Danny, an Elizabethan mansion that was remodelled in the time of Queen Anne. During the First World War the house was leased by Prime Minister Lloyd-George and in 1918 the terms of the Armistice were drawn up here by the War Cabinet.

On the far side of the meadow two stiles bring you to Danny's drive and entrance gate. Keep ahead here for

Wolstonbury Hill

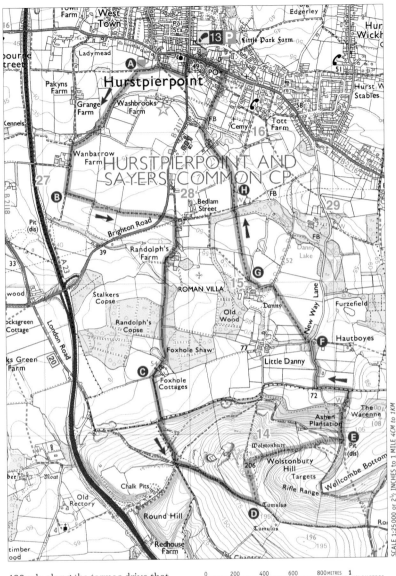

100 yds along the tarmac drive that approaches the north side of the house. Now turn right over a stile, to join the foopath that goes along the edge of the fields and across a plank bridge before dividing at a squeeze stile **G**. Bear right across a meadow and then a field. After a belt of trees there is another plank bridge and a stile. Turn right here, then immediately left to follow the field edge beside fencing to a stile **H**. Cross it and bear left to a further stile a few paces away, now following an enclosed path that reaches a lane at Little Washbrook Farm. Continue for 150 yds then turn right onto a waymarked footpath that crosses a footbridge and driveway and second footbridge before climbing to the village green. Turn left at the main street in order to return to the car park and ultimately the village centre.

The Wey and Arun Canal from Billingshurst

Start	Billingshurst library	GPS waypoints
Distance	6 miles (9.7km)	🖉 TQ 085 260
Height gain	150 feet (45m)	Ⓐ TQ 072 254
		Ⓑ TQ 062 244
Approximate time	3 hours	Ⓒ TQ 058 243
Parking	At start	Ⓓ TQ 058 245
		Ⓔ TQ 066 255
Route terrain	Field and canalside paths	Ⓕ TQ 069 271
Ordnance Survey maps	Landranger 197 (Chichester &	Ⓖ TQ 076 268
	The South Downs), Explorer 134	Ⓗ TQ 080 262
	(Crawley & Horsham)	

There is hardly anything in the way of a gradient in this interesting walk by the upper reaches of the River Arun. The path runs between the river and the towpath of the old Wey and Arun Canal.

Before the coming of the railway, Billingshurst was a busy staging-post on the road between Bognor and London, and several large inns lined the main street. While the railway dealt an initial blow to the fortune of Billingshurst, it later restored its prosperity when commuters began to settle in and around the village. This development has accelerated in recent years, and the walk sets off through the pleasant modern housing that now reaches out to the A29 bypass.

🖉 Start the walk from the library at Billingshurst, on the west side of the large village that is bisected by the Roman Stane Street. Walk away from the main street and pass to the left of the library. Go left at the crossroads and walk down Frenches Mead to the T-junction. Turn right into West Street, then left at the roundabout into Newbridge Road East, and continue across the footbridge over the bypass.

Continue along the redundant highway past Bridgewaters Farm and bear left to join the footpath by the side of the A272. At Lordings Road (B2133) turn left to pass the Victorian postbox and the pantiled **Limeburners Inn**. About 50 yds after the pub, turn right Ⓐ on to the drive to Guildenhurst Manor.

After 100 yds leave the drive to the left through a kissing-gate. A wooden wicket gate now leads you diagonally across a paddock to a gate near its right-hand corner. The enclosed footpath now bears right through a second gate to skirt paddocks and crosses a footbridge at the corner. From here, follow the signposted zigzag left, then right, and continue down the signposted path between hedging and fencing to reach a large pond. Turn right, and follow the water's edge around to the left until you cross the concrete bridge over the outlet stream. Bear right after this to follow the new-born River Arun on a delightful path that gives a distant view of the church at Wisborough Green. Go through a damp meadow full of buttercups to come to a stile just before electricity lines. Keep ahead for 50 yds after this, before bearing left **B** to climb with the cables overhead to the top of the wood.

Turn right on to a grassy path that follows the edge of the wood westwards, enjoying the wide view of richly wooded hills with no habitation in sight until Frithwood Farm appears on the left. Continue to skirt the wood as the path drops to a gateway, beyond which

the footpath divides **C**. Keep right to follow the path that curves right to reach the footbridge and kissing-gate at Lording's Lock. This lock (also known as Orfold Lock) is the top lock of six and from here the barges had to travel another 67 miles to reach London Bridge. The canal crosses the river on an aqueduct just north of the lock, where an information board explains the details and continuing restoration.

Go over the stile after the lock **D** and

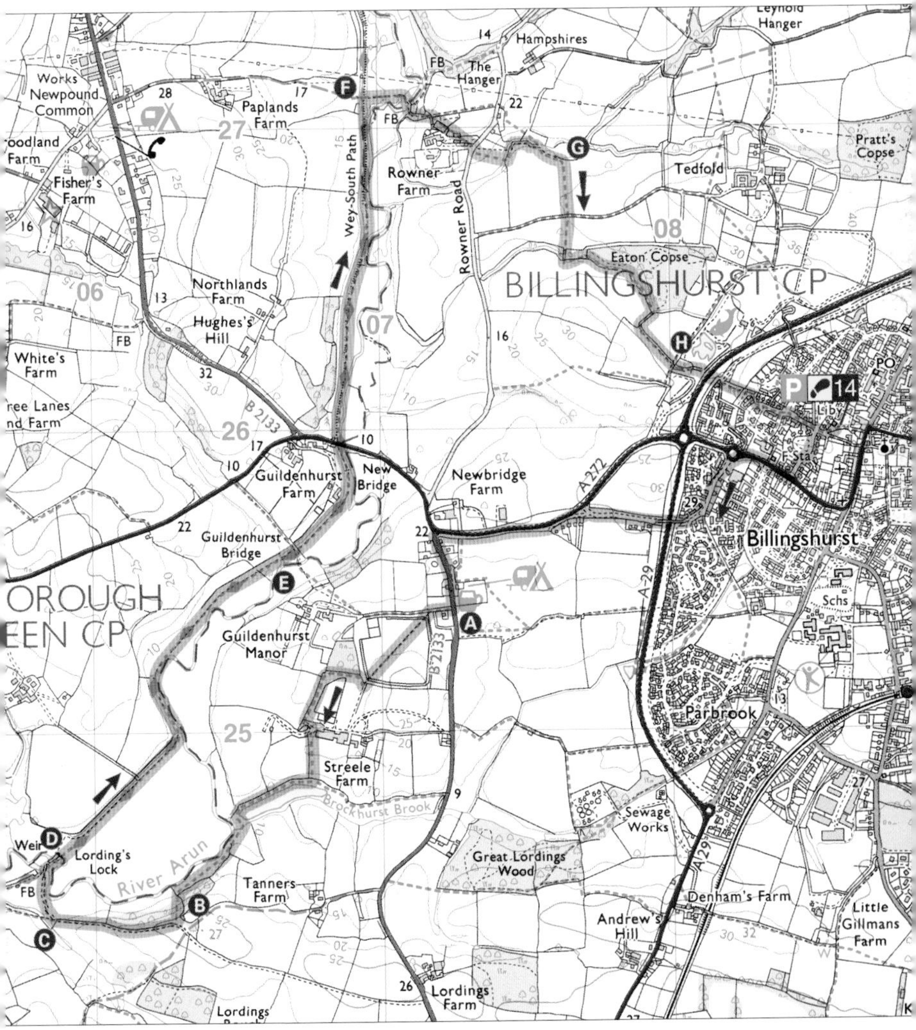

Wey and Arun Canal

Rowner Lock, just before the electricity pylon spanning the canal. Here lock gates have been restored. Cross the River Arun at a sluice and climb the path to the top, bearing left through a farmyard to reach Rowner Road. Cross it to a stile. Cross a field to a footbridge in the left-hand corner. Turn left and walk along the edge of a field to reach a signpost at a junction by three metal gates. Do not go through the gates but keep the wire fence to the left for 100 yds to a signpost **G**.

keep ahead along the left bank of the old canal (if you prefer you can follow a meandering riverside path). Parts of the canal are infilled as the right of way cuts across a wide loop of the river. The path continues over a stile and turns left as it runs between canal and river. After a wooden footbridge, keep ahead **E** – do not cross Guildenhurst Bridge to the right over the Arun – and follow the canal to Newbridge.

Cross the road and continue by the canal – even if you fail to spot a kingfisher, dragonflies and herons should be seen somewhere along this section. The lift bridge at Northlands Farm does not look as though it is operated often, but the memorial stone close by is poignant – 'a place for kingfishers to rest'.

Turn right **F** at a canal bridge by

Turn right across the field to the signpost and stile opposite. Cross a lane and then a meadow; go through a belt of trees and then, before the second gate, turn left at the signpost onto an enclosed footpath by the side of Eaton Copse. Turn right at the footpath sign by the end of the copse and continue through a wooded tunnel for 100 yds. Now turn left over a stile and follow the left-hand hedge down the side of an open field towards new housing.

At a crossways by trees **H**, take the right-hand stile and, keep ahead through woodland to reach the bypass.

Cross the road to the footpath opposite, and after a few paces join another path. Keep left and after a few paces, as the path bends left, go straight on through woodland to pass a children's play area. Continue to a road. Turn left towards the church and cross Coombe Hill to return to Billinghurst Library. ●

Midhurst and Cowdray Park

		GPS waypoints	
Start	Midhurst	🖉	SU 887 217
Distance	6½ miles (10.5km)	Ⓐ	SU 889 213
Height gain	510 feet (155m)	Ⓑ	SU 896 206
Approximate time	3 hours	Ⓒ	SU 903 201
Parking	Car park at northern end of North Street	Ⓓ	SU 910 201
		Ⓔ	SU 917 218
		Ⓕ	SU 918 228
Route terrain	Undulating parkland and farmland paths and tracks	Ⓖ	SU 907 224
		Ⓗ	SU 900 222
Ordnance Survey maps	Landranger 197 (Chichester & The South Downs), Explorer 133 (Haslemere & Petersfield)		

Midhurst is an attractive country town with a wealth of ancient buildings. Although only the earthen mound of its castle remains, the walls of Cowdray are still standing. Cowdray was one of the great palaces of Tudor England, built by the Earl of Southampton in the early 16th century; a fire in 1793 left it uninhabitable. There are fine views of its romantic ruins at the beginning and end of this walk, which also passes through lovely woodland. Cowdray Park, with its golf course, polo field and gallops provides an interesting final section.

🖉 Take the path from the bottom left-hand corner of the car park, which leads to Cowdray. Do not cross the bridge to the ruins but turn right and walk along the western bank of the River Rother, following its meanders until you reach the earthen ramparts of Midhurst Castle. Continue on the riverside path, which ends at a small industrial estate with a pumping station on the left Ⓐ. Keep straight on to cross an ancient bridge.

After the bridge, keep ahead along a path and at a fork, take the right-hand path to a stile. Climb it and continue along a pleasant field edge path with woods to the right. Cross two stiles in quick succession and take the path behind farm buildings to a road. Bear left and descend to a road junction where a bridleway (to Heyshott and Grafham) begins on the opposite side of the T-junction.

Turn left off the main track at a fingerpost Ⓑ and climb steeply up the hill. The antiquity of this track is soon apparent: it is deeply cut into the hillside with overhanging trees. You may well catch sight of deer. After the initial steep climb the track follows an up-and-down course. Carry straight on when another bridleway joins from the left. The track soon becomes more level and sandy as it passes a plantation of conifers and crosses the aptly named Todham Rough. Turn left where the track meets another bridleway at a T-junction **C** and then take the first turning on the right.

The way now goes through chestnut woods, sheltering an abundance of game birds. Go straight on when the path bends right and follow the path downhill and round to the left **D**. Pass a path on the right. Follow the edge of the woods to a cottage. From here the track is surfaced and it soon meets Selham Road.

Turn left onto the narrow lane and after 250 yds, by a solitary oak, turn right onto a path across fields. The path drops down to the River Rother and cuts between trees and the field edge to a stile. Climb it and follow a path across a field to reach the road at Ambersham Bridge.

Cross the bridge and follow the lane, crossing straight over when it meets with the main Petworth to Midhurst road (A272) to a sunken path opposite **E**. An enjoyable short stretch climbing through woods ends where the path meets a lane at the top. Turn right and then after walking 100 yds turn left and then immediately right. A fork is seen here. Take the left turning, following the bridleway along the western side of Heathend Copse. Note that the right-of-way lies inside the wood and is not the track on the edge of the field. Here too

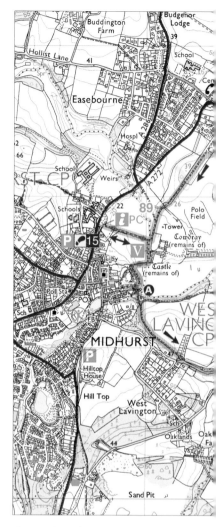

there are large flocks of tame pheasants. Just before the end of the copse a footpath leaves to the left **F**. Take this to cross to the plantation opposite and then turn left onto the path along its edge. At the end of the copse the right-of-way strikes south west across Cowdray Park. The tiny Steward's Pond soon comes into view, and the path skirts the southern

Cowdray

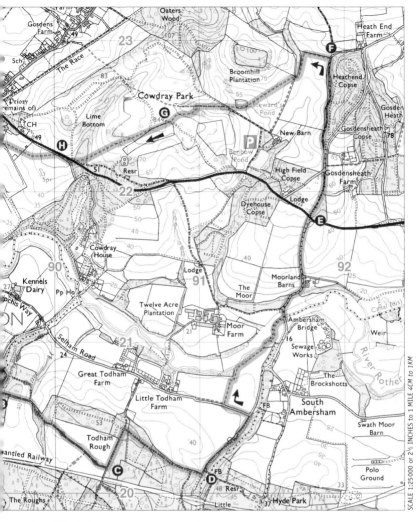

edge of this before it crosses a pony track and climbs a declivity on the edge of the golf course. Keep trees and bushes on the right and cross a fairway to a shelter opposite **G**. Now head downhill, with a fairway to the left, keeping to the rough ground. Make for an enormous oak tree and watch out for golf balls in flight. From the large oak you will see a group of trees farther on and a signpost to the road. When you get to the road, turn right and walk along it to the top of the hill where a kissing-gate on the left **H** gives access to a field.

Walk diagonally across the pasture making for the right of Midhurst – Cowdray is clearly visible from here. A stile comes into view along this stretch. Cross it and walk across the field to a gate in the far left corner. Follow the enclosed path ahead between trees and the polo field to a track, running from Easebourne into Midhurst, and turn left.

When you come to the ruins of Cowdray turn right and cross the bridge onto a path which leads back to the starting point. ●

Belloc's Mill

		GPS waypoints
Start	School Lane, Shipley	✐ TQ 143 219
Distance	6 miles (9.7km). Shorter version 5½ miles (8.9km)	Ⓐ TQ 144 219 Ⓑ TQ 153 218
Height gain	180 feet (55m). Shorter version 130 feet (40m)	Ⓒ TQ 155 212 Ⓓ TQ 147 213
Approximate time	3 hours. (2½ hours for shorter version)	Ⓔ TQ 149 204 Ⓕ TQ 151 196
Parking	Roadside village car park at start, 100 yds east of the King's Mill entrance	Ⓖ TQ 134 194 Ⓗ TQ 137 207
Route terrain	Undulating farmland and parkland paths	
Ordnance Survey maps	Landranger 198 (Brighton & Lewes), Explorers 134 (Crawley & Horsham) and 121 (Arundel & Pulborough)	

Start the walk by King's Mill (bought by the writer Hilaire Belloc in 1906) and then continue with an exploration of the surrounding countryside. Some of the bridleways are muddy most of the year so this is not a walk for those wearing trainers.

Built in 1879, the King's Mill at Shipley is one of the finest working smock mills in the country. The term comes from the shape of the tower, supposed to resemble the garment traditionally worn by country workers of the time. The fantail, set at right angles to the main sails, moves the cap to keep the sails facing the wind. Belloc lived in Shipley and bought the mill, which continued to work until 1926 – the beginning of the agricultural depression. The author still owned it when he died in 1953, by which time it was in disrepair. The windmill was restored as a memorial to Belloc, and its sails began turning again in 1958.

✐ Turn east along School Lane, then left at the junction into Red Lane. Just beyond Kings Platt, the group of modern houses and bungalows to the right, turn off the road to the right Ⓐ onto a footpath running down the side of a meadow by the gardens of houses. After 100 yds go right again through a kissing-gate into a wood. A stile takes the path on into another meadow. Go along the left-hand side to an iron gate giving onto a lane. Cross to a footpath that goes through a belt of trees into a meadow and follow a line of old oak trees to reach a fingerpost on the far side. Turn right onto a drive and after 300 yds, by a corner of a wood Ⓑ, leave the drive to the right to cross a large field to reach the main drive coming from Knepp Castle, a gothic fantasy complete with turrets and battlements. The scant remains of its Norman predecessor can be seen by the A24. King John later enjoyed staying at the castle, using it as a hunting lodge and keeping 200 greyhounds there for pursuing deer.

Turn right onto the drive by an enormous oak tree and leave the park by New Lodge. Continue along the drive for ¼ mile to take the footpath to the right **C**, immediately before the converted Charlwood Barn. However, you may like to keep on the drive for a few more yards to see beautiful Kneppmill Pond to the left before returning to take the footpath. The pond is one of the largest hammer ponds in the county and served Knepp Furnace from 1568 until iron-making ended there in 1604.

The footpath follows the left-hand side of the field. There are more magnificent oak trees to the left (a memorable feature of this walk and descendants of those that fed the furnace)

and extensive views. Go over a plank bridge at the corner of the field and cross a narrow meadow to a more substantial bridge spanning the River Adur. Once there was a causeway across the water meadow here, but only fragments of timber and brickwork remain. The clear path continues ahead across the field – ignore the alternative to the left – and turn right through the gate onto Swallows Lane.

Turn left at Pound Corner **D** onto the footpath that follows a concrete track

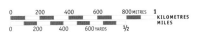

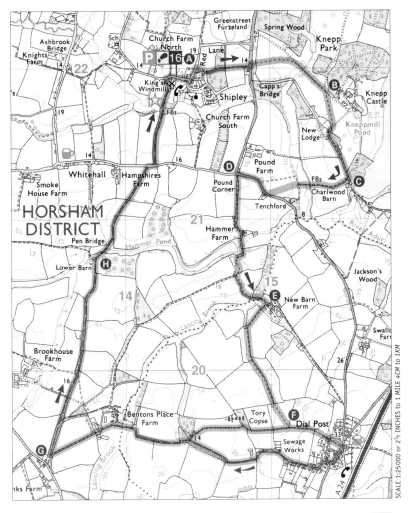

King's Mill at Shipley – once owned by Hilaire Belloc

Soon habitation is left behind, and the lane becomes a quiet byway.

The short-cut avoiding Dial Post rejoins just before a half-hidden house at the corner of a wood.

After the house the track divides. Keep left and continue – the bridleway has now become a lovely green way. At Bentons Place Farm keep the farmhouse to the right and stay on the main track for ¼ mile to come to trees where it swings left.

A few paces after the bend, turn right over a plank bridge **G** and after a few paces turn right to join a bridleway heading north east.

In summer this is the most delightful part of the route with a breathtaking display of wild flowers and butterflies and delicious blackberries. Keep ahead along the broad bridleway until a metal gate across the track heralds the cattle shelter at Lower Barn. Walk past the shelter and turn right into a narrower track **H**. Even in summer the going may be muddy here at times, and in dry conditions the mud becomes well rutted. On reaching the lane, you may like to turn left for a 750-yd diversion to the **Countryman Inn**. Otherwise turn right for 50 yds, then left to rejoin the bridleway. Continue across a footbridge to reach Shipley Mill, where you bear left onto the tarmac drive for the return to School Lane. Turn right for the final 100 yds back to the car park. ●

towards Hammer Barn. The concrete surface ends at Hammer Farm; follow the gravel lane as it heads south beyond the farm, then bear left at the next footpath junction and continue to New Barn Farm **E**.

Turn right opposite an asbestos shed, to pass a pond. Bear left after a galvanised gate to follow a fingerpost and walk along the edge of a field with a hedge to the left. Continue through a gate along the edge of a much larger field, still following the hedge on your left. Cross the next one to a plank bridge **F** and turn left to Dial Post *(or turn right if you do not wish to visit the village).*

Go through a gate and over two stiles. Cross the village green to the main street, turning right to pass the **Crown inn**. After 150 yds, turn right into Bentons Lane and fork left at Half Acre.

Selsey and Pagham Harbour

		GPS waypoints
Start	Selsey	🖊 SZ 865 933
Distance	7½ miles (12.1km)	Ⓐ SZ 863 940
Height gain	Negligible	Ⓑ SZ 873 949
Approximate time	3 hours	Ⓒ SZ 856 962
Parking	East Beach car park	Ⓓ SZ 848 947
Route terrain	Residential roads and tracks, well-used paths across fields and marshes	Ⓔ SZ 852 936
Ordnance Survey maps	Landranger 197 (Chichester & the South Downs), Explorer 120 (Chichester)	

At times quite bracing, this spectacular coastal walk begins by heading for the desolate and highly evocative marshes to the south of Pagham Harbour. For about two miles, the path runs directly along the edge of the harbour before heading across expansive, prairie-like farmland in the direction of Selsey. The last leg cuts through the town and then along the sea front.

In ancient times Selsey was part of a small island. Today, the town is still almost entirely enclosed by water. Situated at the southern tip of a promontory, Selsey faces the English Channel to the south east and south west, while Pagham Harbour lies to the north east and a brook, known as the Broad Rife, to the north west. It was once a sizeable town, with many historic buildings and a cathedral. The sea, sadly, has engulfed much of it, over the centuries.

🖊 From the car park cross over to a tarmac path and follow it round the side of a pond. At the road turn left and then immediately right. Pass Marisfield Place, and then turn right into Manor Lane. Follow it into Drift Road and at the far end, on the north-east edge of Selsey, continue ahead on a waymarked track Ⓐ. Pass beside the buildings of Park Farm and continue on the track

across the fields. When you reach a gate and footpath sign by a ditch, go round the side of the gate and then follow the path along the left-hand edge of the field towards a house with a conservatory. Turn right at the house, walk along the field boundary and pass a memorial stone to Kitty Child.

The next stage of the walk is across a marshy coastal landscape far removed from the bungalows and seaside attractions of Selsey only a stone's throw away. Turn left on reaching a waymark Ⓑ to join a shingle path and follow it with the coast away to the right and reed beds on the left. Soon you merge with a clearer coastal path. After several minutes veer half left down some old railway sleepers and follow the path along the edge of Pagham Harbour. On reaching a path on the left, follow it to a drive and the 13th-century Chapel of St Wilfrid at

Church Norton on the right.

Pass through the churchyard to a seat at the far end and a stile in the wall. Cross it and follow the path, skirting the field edge. Avoid steps on the right and continue along the upper path, which has a footpath–no cycling sign. Rejoin the harbour edge, turn left and soon return to the parallel path running across the marshes.

Pagham Harbour provides ornithologists with the opportunity to spot waders – especially in winter. Redshanks, curlews, grey plovers and godwits are a common sight here. Swans may also be seen on this stretch and often there is the salty tang of the sea on the breeze, reminding you that the English Channel is only a stone's throw away.

Eventually the path curves right and as it does so, go straight on and out to the B2145 road . Cross it with care and as the road curves left, veer right opposite Ferry Farmhouse. Go through a gate and across the field towards some derelict buildings. Beyond the buildings follow the track round to the left where

Boats drawn up on the shore at Selsey

there is a faint track on the right. Avoid it, continue to a T-junction and turn right, passing a turning on the left. Keep ahead to the field corner, turn right at the waymark and then at the next corner swing left. Follow the field edge with the fairways of a golf club on the left.

Pass a path on the right and at the next footpath sign, turn left to pass alongside holiday caravans and chalets . The track becomes a tarmac drive, passes Northcommon Farm on the right and then reaches the entrance to the golf club. At this point swing right to join Paddock Lane, following it through the caravan park. Head for the junction with Horsefield Road and continue straight ahead. At length the road bends sharply round to the right to a junction. Turn left for a few yards, then left again (signposted The Forge). On reaching Selsey High Street, turn right, then left after a few paces to follow Latham Road all the way to a T-junction.

Cross over on to a tarmac path, then cross another road to follow a path between hedging and fencing. Turn right by **the Lifeboat** pub and walk along towards the seafront. On reaching

it, head towards the Lifeboat Station and Museum. Follow the paved promenade with the sea on the right. After about ½ mile, when you reach a children's play area on the left, leave the shore path and head across to the car park where the walk began. ●

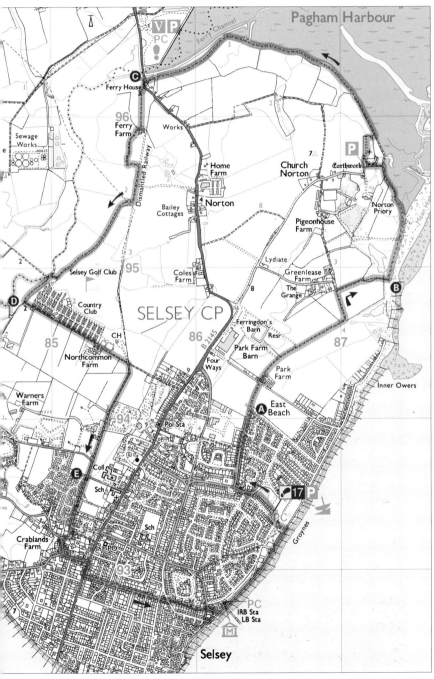

Arundel Park and South Stoke

		GPS waypoints
Start	Arundel	
Distance	7¼ miles (11.6km)	✎ TQ 020 070
Height gain	625 feet (190m)	Ⓐ TQ 013 073
		Ⓑ TQ 016 077
Approximate time	3½ hours	Ⓒ TQ 012 094
Parking	Mill Road car park	Ⓓ TQ 014 102
		Ⓔ TQ 025 099
Route terrain	Parkland and riverside paths	
Ordnance Survey maps	Landranger 197 (Chichester & The South Downs), Explorer 121 (Arundel & Pulborough)	

This lovely walk begins under the walls of Arundel Castle and then passes through the impressive park which surrounds the castle, the home of the dukes of Norfolk for 500 years. The return part of the route follows the course of the River Arun eastwards and southwards, at first through rich woodland high on a cliff overlooking the valley and then on the banks of the river itself. Note that dogs are restricted to public rights-of-way in Arundel Park which is closed annually on 24 March. However, the route of this walk is unaffected.

Castle, church and Catholic cathedral perched above a bend in the river give Arundel a continental air. The juxta-position of the buildings reflects the uneasy relationship that existed from the Reformation to the present century between the mainly Protestant towns-people and the Catholic dukes of Norfolk, owners of the castle and premier peers of the realm.

The extensive walls and towers of Arundel Castle make a splendid sight. It is mainly a 19th-century reconstruction of the original Norman castle but some earlier work remains, including the 11th-century shell keep. Close by is the medieval church, unique in that the nave is Anglican and the east end Catholic. For a long time the two parts were walled off

from each other but now they are separated by a glass screen that can be opened on ecumenical occasions. The cathedral, an imposing building in the French Gothic style, was erected by a duke of Norfolk in the late 19th century only after the Catholic Church in England was allowed to organise itself into dioceses.

✎ From the car park, turn left and then right when you reach the High Street. The tourist information centre is on the left side of the High Street, which climbs steeply past the medieval parish church on the right and the Catholic cathedral on the left. Opposite a primary school on the left, bear right to enter Arundel Park Ⓐ.

Follow the driveway into the park

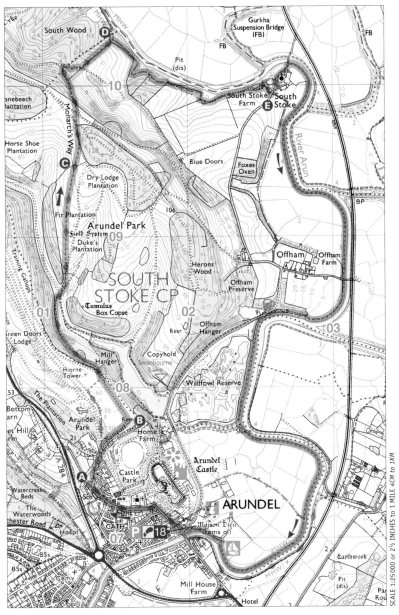

through a kissing-gate by a road gate. Bear right at a notice 'No unauthorised vehicles beyond this point' onto a track and continue, with the Hiorne Tower – built by Francis Hiorne in 1790 – to your left. Cross the end of the gallop (look out for racehorses here), then turn left **B**. On your left can be seen some of the extensive re-afforestation that has been

carried out following the devastation of the 1987 storm. Continue along the track skirting a wood on the right to a field gate and stile. The track then begins a descent into a steep-sided dry valley. This part of the walk is a delight with a wide view of

SCALE 1:25000 or 2½ INCHES to 1 MILE 4CM to 1KM

the park to the right and woods to the left.

At the bottom of the valley, at a major intersection, cross over to an immediate fork and take the left-hand turning, climbing steeply to a stile. Continue ahead on the Monarch's Way, passing a footpath sign. Make for the left edge of Dry Lodge Plantation and keep going to a stile by a clump of trees nearest the wood **C**. Once over the stile continue on the trail, soon merging with a track running along the western edge of the plantation.

The Arun Valley from the north edge of Arundel Park

Walk along the track here, enjoying the fine view on the left towards Duchess Lodge; behind is another splendid panorama – on a clear day you can see the Isle of Wight beyond Chichester harbour. The view ahead opens up at the top of the plantation, where the track sweeps left. Go straight ahead here, following the direction of the Monarch's Way waymark. Head across the grass and look for a distant chalky cliff. You soon come to a stile by a gate, which is another excellent vantage point for vistas over the Arun Valley. Follow the track down and round to the right.

Turn left at the Monarch's Way sign to leave the track and follow a faint path down by a fence, which leads into dense woodland. This becomes steep and dark and there is an old flint wall on the right. Go through a gate in this at the bottom to reach the bridleway **D** which follows the south bank of the River Arun. Take a few steps to the left to view the river or turn sharp right to begin the return leg of the walk.

The bridleway twists its way through woodland which screens views of the river, and eventually it climbs through the wood to reach the top of a cliff. Another climb later follows, and the track becomes a field edge path leading into South Stoke. Turn right to pass behind a cart shed, which used to have accommodation for labourers on its upper floor, and reach the lane **E** into the hamlet. Turn left here to visit the unpretentious and utterly peaceful little St Leonard's Church, its interior dominated by an enormous cast iron stove. It is usually open. Continue down the lane (footpath and farm track only signs) to the bridge and turn right along the path on the west bank of the river.

The walking now is undemanding, the tranquility disturbed only by the passing of a train or, rarely, a boat. You may see herons here and some less common waterbirds. Burpham church can be seen nestling among trees as a navigational cut truncates the eastern meander of the river. The dramatic silhouette of Arundel Castle appears as the footpath approaches a cattle bridge across the river at Offham Farm, but the apparent distance to Arundel is deceptive since the river makes another meander eastwards before reaching the town. Before this final section the riverside path passes the **Black Rabbit pub**. The path ends back at Mill Road car park. ●

The Temple of the Winds from Fernhurst

		GPS waypoints
Start	Fernhurst	
Distance	6¼ miles (10km)	SU 896 284
Height gain	1,000 feet (305m)	**A** SU 902 296
Approximate time	3½ hours	**B** SU 906 305
		C SU 906 313
Parking	Car park off Vann Road in the centre of Fernhurst	**D** SU 912 305
		E SU 918 301
		F SU 920 302
Route terrain	Meandering paths and tracks through thickly wooded hill country	**G** SU 914 289
		H SU 906 286
Ordnance Survey maps	Landranger 186 (Aldershot & Guildford) and 197 (Chichester & The South Downs), Explorer 133 (Haslemere & Petersfield)	

The Temple of the Winds was a summerhouse built at the summit of Blackdown by Alfred, Lord Tennyson when he lived at nearby Aldworth House. The summerhouse has gone but the viewpoint remains. At 919 feet (280m) it is the highest point in the county.

Cross the main road at Fernhurst (A286) into Church Road and pass the church, which was virtually rebuilt by Anthony Salvin, a local resident, in the 19th century. Continue to the green and turn left towards **the Red Lion**. At the junction in front of it, turn left and head up the slope. Follow the road and as it bends left towards the main road, take the path on the right. Follow it between gardens and soon cross a stile to skirt a field before reaching the next stile. Cross a tarmac drive and continue ahead in the next field. Make for a stile at the top and keep ahead in the next pasture. When you reach another tarmac drive, keep right, at the sign for 'Copyhold'. Beyond a house take the path on the right, over a stile **A**. The path descends to the bottom of the valley, and there are ponds to the right.

The climb, to the other side of the valley, is steep. Bear right at the top to climb a low bank and join a bridleway. Turn left onto the grassy track, pausing to look back at the fine view.

Farther on, avoid a bridleway sign and a path running down to a tarmac drive and continue on the path parallel to it. On reaching the drive, turn right and walk along to the road by a sign for Sheetlands. Turn left here and, immediately after the gate to Wadesmarsh Farmhouse, leave the road to the right **B** to enter the National Trust's Valewood Park. The parkland provides lovely walking with the house and lake to the right and specimen trees ahead. The path joins the drive from the house. After 120 yds leave the drive to the right for a footpath that climbs steps to a kissing-gate. At the top of the field

C turn right to go through a gate and walk below the trees to a gate that is above cattle sheds and leads into the woods.

The path goes up through trees to a kissing-gate and footpath sign. Head straight on across the field, keeping trees on the right. Go through a gate by a sign for Valewood Park and follow the Sussex Border Path, following a path made gloomy by overhanging rhododendrons. Go through a gate at a Sussex Border Path fingerpost and continue for some time on the trail. Pass a waymark for the Serpent Trail and continue over a bridleway crossing **D**.

This is Black Down. After about ½ mile the path descends to a junction **E**. Keep left, avoiding a path on the extreme left, pass a sunken path on the right and when you reach several pools, turn right onto a bridleway. Keep right immediately onto another bridleway **F**.

Take the left fork and continue through the trees. Pass a path merging from the right and then steps leading off to the left before taking a path signposted Temple of the Winds. This path leads to the memorial seat to Mabel, wife of Edward Hunter, who gave Black Down to the National Trust in 1944. This was the site of the summerhouse erected by Tennyson during the 24 years that he occupied Aldworth House, the home he built a

A stunning view from the site of The Temple of the Winds

mile or so to the north. Remarkably this was open country until 1958 when the National Trust began to plant conifers.

Walk clockwise around the summit to pass a strategically placed rustic seat, pausing to enjoy the beautiful view, and then bear left on to a path that descends the spur to the south-west, between high banks. Turn right when it reaches a lane, but after a few yards go left down a bridleway track **G** which soon swings right. After a house, keep left at a junction on a path that leads down into woodland and that has at least a trickle of water flowing down most of the year.

Cross a track and continue down the mossy-banked path, which merges with a waymarked track farther down. Keep ahead and at the point where it reaches a lane, at Tanyard Cottage **H**, turn right on to a path into woodland, with the stream to the right. Bear right to walk with a field, and then Fernhurst's cricket ground, to the left. The path emerges into the village next to the Red Lion inn. Retrace your steps to the A286.

SCALE 1:25 000 or 2½ INCHES to 1 MILE 4CM to 1KM

0   200   400   600   800 METRES   1
                                     KILOMETRES
                                     MILES
0   200   400   600 YARDS   ½

THE TEMPLE OF THE WINDS FROM FERNHURST ● 59

Woolbeding Common and Hammer Wood

		GPS waypoints
Start	Woolbeding Common viewpoint	⬦ SU 869 260
Distance	7¼ miles (11.6km)	Ⓐ SU 865 261
Height gain	985 feet (300m)	Ⓑ SU 860 258
Approximate time	3½ hours	Ⓒ SU 851 256
Parking	Car park just before end of public road to Woolbeding Common	Ⓓ SU 839 250
		Ⓔ SU 830 247
Route terrain	Demanding walking through extensive woodland	Ⓕ SU 843 238
		Ⓖ SU 855 234
Ordnance Survey maps	Landranger 197 (Chichester & The South Downs), Explorer 133 (Haslemere & Petersfield)	Ⓗ SU 856 240
		Ⓙ SU 862 248

Woolbeding is a tiny village close to Midhurst, with a church where services are held by candlelight. The walk blends airy heath with shady forest and passes a large hammer pond, a reminder that the district was once an important centre of the iron industry. Note the precipitous slope between Ⓔ and Ⓕ, which may be dangerous when wet.

⬦ From the car park, turn right along the lane, pausing to admire the view to the west and north that takes in much of three counties. After 300 yds turn left off the road where a footpath crosses by a seat. Do not take the path that descends steeply from here but turn right to follow the ridge for about 150 yds past a triangulation pillar hidden in the bushes just off the path. Now turn left onto the waymarked Serpent Trail and drop down to a bench seat and three-way fingerpost. Take the second turning on the right (signposted Serpent Trail and public footpath), and contour along the foot of the ridge to a crossways Ⓐ at Barnett's Cottage.

Bear left past the house, to pass a second house on your left. Cross its drive, and descend with a fence on your

left to cross two drives at Honeysuckle Cottage; now the waymarked path makes its way down through holly and oak woods to Linch Road. Take the footpath opposite that goes through woods before coming to a level, marshy area where there is a crossways. Keep ahead to come to a waymarked junction **B**. Enter the trees and walk ahead for a few paces to where you see a second waymark. Keep left here, still following the Serpent Trail. Follow the path to a T-junction and turn left. The path climbs gently through bracken to reach a driveway at Titty Hill.

Turn left and, where the surfaced road begins, fork left into the woods again. Leave the woods by a stile and follow a track behind the houses at Queen's Corner. Bear left by a garage to resume on a footpath at the entrance to Brandon Beeches. Cross the bottom of the field here to a T-junction. Turn left, then turn right over the stile at the edge of the woods **C** to walk westwards, with a fine view to the right.

At the end of the woods, follow a

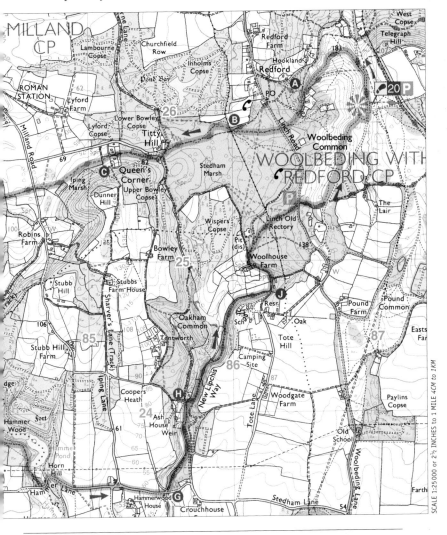

churchyard wall to the stile on Milland Road (note that the church has been demolished). Cross the road to a second stile, then go across a pasture to a plank bridge and the stile leading into Kingsham Wood.

Keep the fence on your left, and follow the obvious path past a fingerpost by a large beech tree. The way drops down to join a woodland track, and a stile takes the right of way out of the woods and into a field. Bear right to cross it to reach a stile in the corner **D** and turn right on to a track. Follow it to a road junction.

Take the road signposted to Borden Wood – Jungle Wood is to the right with its inappropriate pine trees. After ¼ mile, where the road begins to climb more steeply, turn left onto a footpath and climb away from the road for 180 yds.

Leave the Serpent Trail here, and turn left onto a footpath **E** that climbs steeply (but briefly) after branching right from the main track. Swing right at the top and then left after a few paces on to Green Lane. Follow it and at length reach a road. Turn right along it for a few yards. Take the footpath on the left keeping close to the fence, trees and bushes on the left, to reach the corner of the field. The path then descends a short but steep slope, veers to the right, and takes the left-hand fork along a ledge. The trail falls gently and then rises again, all the while clinging precariously to a precipitous slope. The final stretch is down a steep slope that would need great care in the wet. Turn right on to the sunken track at the bottom to reach a lane.

Walk for a few yards along the lane before turning left into the woods **F** belonging to Chithurst Forest Monastery. This section makes particularly pleasant walking, and the sweet chestnuts would be a bonus in autumn. There are

The view before **F**

glimpses of Hammer Pond as the path dips down to its southern end (there will probably be muddy patches here). Turn left when the path reaches Hammer Lane. On a hot day the shady coolness of the sunken byway is welcome. Cross Iping Lane onto the lane to Hammerwood, another ancient, sunken lane. Cross the stream at the bottom and then turn left **G** to climb into the wood. A mossy wall is soon close to the left and there is a beautiful long meadow beyond it. At the entrance to Ash House take the drive to the right at the sign and, just before reaching a house where the track swings left, look to the right to see a narrow sunken path **H** climbing into the wood.

This path takes you to a bridleway, keep left and pass a track running down to a gate with a pond beyond. Climb steadily to a T-junction **J**. Go left and keep ahead when the surfaced road ends. Bear right when the track divides after Woolhouse Farm and then, at a complicated four-way junction, take the path that goes half-right into the woods. Cross the road to re-enter Woolbeding Common. The path climbs steadily to the lane but, instead of joining it at this point, it is more enjoyable to use one of the paths that wind across the heathland, roughly parallel to the lane, to return to the car park. ●

Amberley and Parham House

Start	Kithurst Hill, off the B2139 near Storrington
Distance	7¾ miles (12.4km)
Height gain	805 feet (245m)
Approximate time	4 hours
Parking	At start
Route terrain	Parkland and field paths and undulating stretch of the South Downs Way
Ordnance Survey maps	Landranger 197 (Chichester & the South Downs), Explorer 121 (Arundel & Pulborough)

GPS waypoints

◢ TQ 070 124
Ⓐ TQ 070 130
Ⓑ TQ 070 145
Ⓒ TQ 046 144
Ⓓ TQ 031 129
Ⓔ TQ 050 125

The South Downs Way to the south and south west of Storrington offers magnificent views of the West Sussex countryside and coast. From this high ground, the walk immediately descends to the road and then meanders through the very English surroundings of Parham Park before cutting across country to the picturesque village of Amberley. Finally, and perhaps best of all, comes that scenic stretch along the South Downs Way, back to the start.

◢ Starting in the car park, make for the vehicular exit and bend left for several paces. With a track running in from the right, join a signposted bridleway running off down the hill to a wooden gate. Go diagonally down the pasture to the next gate and then on down through the woods, at one point turning sharp right to follow the sunken path through the trees. Merge with a track by a galvanised gate and soon you reach a waymark Ⓐ. Follow the grassy track along the left edge of the field; looking back at this stage reveals a broad curtain of woodland through which the walk has just passed. Make for the field corner by a bungalow and turn right at the road.

After about 50 yds turn left into Clay Lane, following it between hedgerows. Pass Cootham Farmhouse on the left and cut through trees to a T-junction. This is the A283. Just visible to the right, a few hundred yards away, is the **Crown Inn**. However, the main walk turns left along the road. As it curves right, head straight on Ⓑ along the public footpath towards Parham House. Follow the West Sussex Literary Trail through the estate, go through a gate by a lodge and continue on the drive as it curves left. At this point there is a teasing glimpse of the escarpment of the South Downs. A footpath waymark also looms into view here; follow the grassy path ahead, parallel to the main drive. Pass through a smattering of trees and then cross open parkland to the next

On Rackham Hill

drive. A dovecote and the outline of Parham House are seen over to the left.

This splendid Elizabethan mansion is acknowledged as one of the great historic gems of Sussex. Queen Elizabeth I is thought to have dined here in 1593, en route to Cowdray from Sutton Park in Surrey. During the Second World War, 30 child evacuees from South London were billeted at Parham. The 875-acre estate was first opened to the public in 1948 – one of the first of Britain's stately homes to be given tourist attraction status.

Follow the drive ahead, passing a stone wall and a lake and continue to a pair of lodges and a kissing-gate leading out to the road. Turn left and proceed to a junction with a turning for Greatham and Cold Waltham. Turn right into Greatham Road for several paces, then swing left opposite a bungalow to join a woodland path. Pass through bracken and holly trees, descend to a junction with a house to the right and turn right to rejoin the West Sussex Literary Trail. Make for the corner of the wood, where there is a footbridge on the left **C**.

Cross it and head south on a grassy path alongside fencing. Cross a stile, pass between a house and Rackham Mill to the next stile and follow the woodland path to a footbridge and stile. Continue ahead to the next bridge and stile, then cut diagonally across the field to a plank bridge spanning a ditch. Cross a grassy track to a gap in the hedge, then a fourth footbridge before heading up a large field towards trees. At the road turn right and walk into Amberley. Pass the **Sportsman** pub on the right and continue with grand views of the South Downs. In the village centre follow the road round to the left by **the Black Horse** and continue through Amberley, passing between scores of picturesque cottages, ancient timber-framed buildings and handsome period houses.

Situated on a plateau overlooking the Arun Valley, Amberley is often described as 'the pearl of Sussex'. There are plenty of attractions and you can see the village more than justifies its name. Among

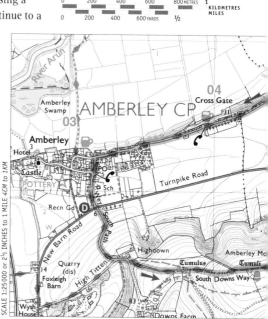

other features is imposing Amberley Castle, which dates back to Norman times and was strongly fortified by Bishop Rede in 1377. Originally it was the residence of the Bishops of Chichester. However, Amberley's fate was sealed when the Parliamentarians began to dismantle it during the Civil War, though parts of the castle still survive today, having been cleverly converted into a luxury hotel.

The walk now coincides with the route of the Wey South Path. Pass the village school and proceed to the junction with Turnpike Road **D**. Cross over into Mill Lane and head uphill through trees. Pass Mill Lane Cottage and continue up the lane between hedgerows to a junction with the South Downs Way. Keep left here, pass a house called 'Highdown' and avoid a footpath on the right. Follow the lane to the right

and then veer off left at the South Downs Way sign. Climb a bank to a gate and continue on the trail, following it between fences with magnificent views in all directions. Disregard a right of way running off sharp right and keep ahead. When the track divides after about 60 yds, keep left on the South Downs Way and follow it up the steep slope to a gate.

Continue between fencing; over to the right are views of the Sussex coast around Worthing and Littlehampton. Keep ahead to a bridleway crossing **E** and continue on the South Downs Way towards Rackham Hill. A triangulation pillar is visible in the field to the right of the path. Down to the left is Parham House. Merge with a byway running in from the right, pass through a wood and head over Springhead Hill, back to the car park where the walk began. ●

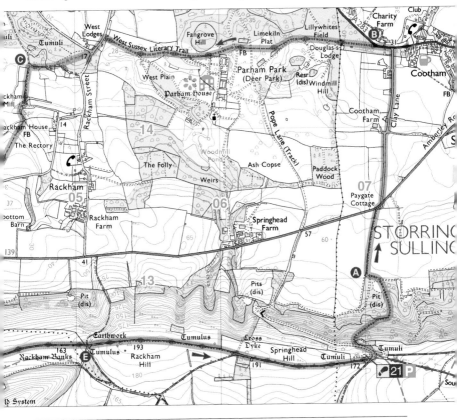

South Harting to the Downs

Start	Harting Downs, off the B2141
Distance	7¾ miles (12.4km)
Height gain	1,130 feet (345m)
Approximate time	4 hours
Parking	At start
Route terrain	Field paths and bridleways, steep but exhilarating sections of the South Downs Way
Ordnance Survey maps	Landranger 197 (Chichester & the South Downs), Explorer 120 (Chichester)

GPS waypoints

- ✏ SU 789 181
- Ⓐ SU 784 194
- Ⓑ SU 789 195
- Ⓒ SU 802 191
- Ⓓ SU 823 185
- Ⓔ SU 820 178
- Ⓕ SU 803 185

This spectacular walk starts appropriately in high downland country. Beyond the village of South Harting the route sticks mainly to low-level footpaths and bridleways before climbing dramatically to the South Downs Way. The last mile or so represents walking on the South Downs at its most glorious, with wonderful views and some stiff climbing giving the experience a real sense of adventure.

🥾 From the car park walk across the open grass space, heading downhill to the waymark. Follow the path into the trees and down to the B2141. Cross over and continue on the South Downs Way. Cut through woodland to the next road, cross it to the restricted byway and as the South Downs Way bears left, go straight on at a sign for South Harting. Keep right at the waymarked fork and at the next fork, where the road is visible, keep ahead. Bear right at the next T-junction and follow the path beside South Harting's recreation ground. At the road, walk ahead through the village. Pass the church on the left

Ⓐ and head down the High Street. On the left is the **White Hart** and ahead at

the bottom is **the Ship**.

This pub is where the writer Hilaire Belloc finished his walk across Sussex at the start of the 20th century, later publishing an account of his journey under the title *The Four Men*. In the book, Belloc is rightly fearful that the world he cherishes is about to change.

Take the road round to the right, walk along to Mill Lane on the left and follow it to a waymarked path on the right. Go up steps into a field **B** and follow the broad path ahead. From here there are glorious views of the South Downs. Make for the field corner and pass through a copse into the next pasture via a gate. Continue to the next gate and over a stile to the road.

Cross it and continue ahead on the footpath, keeping hedge on the right. Farther on the path passes along the left edge of an apple orchard before reaching a gate. Go through it and pass between farm outbuildings to the next road. Cross over at the fork and follow the road signposted Rogate. Turn right between Hamesford House and Marden Farm to follow a signposted footpath. Veer right on reaching farm outbuildings, keeping barns to the left and soon crossing a stile over to the right. Go diagonally across the pasture to the next stile and in the next field continue obliquely through crops on a clear path. On reaching the road, opposite a bus stop and lane, turn left and immediately pass a left turning. Swing right at a bridleway sign to join a track **C**, which soon curves left. Follow the track and with woodland directly on the right, the footpath and bridleway run in tandem. Continue along the edge of farmland and almost at a field corner, turn left at a waymark to a track on a bend. Turn right and after a few paces it bends right.

At this point go straight on along the bridleway, following the track along the field edge with trees to the left. In a small thicket, turn right towards a shaded, enclosed path and then turn

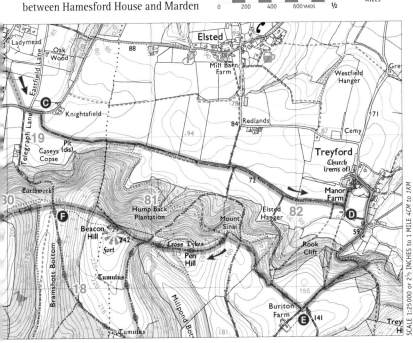

SCALE 1:25000 or 2½ INCHES to 1 MILE 4CM to 1KM

immediately left, keeping barbed wire fencing on the right. Keep ahead until you reach two galvanised gates with Manor Farm seen to the left. Continue on the bridleway, keeping wooden fence on the right, and then turn left at a stile **D**. Head towards Manor Farm, cross a stile in the field corner and keep to the right of a large barn. Go through a gate and walk ahead to the road. Turn sharp right and head downhill, passing the remains of Treyford church among the trees on the right.

This historically significant church is thought to date from the 11th century with 13th-century alterations. It was replaced by another church in 1849 and has been in a dilapidated state of repair for many years. However, in recent times English Heritage has come to its aid and is helping with its restoration.

Follow the lane round the right-hand bend, avoid a bridleway on the right and as the road swings left (signposted Didling and Cocking), keep right to join a no through road. Begin climbing and follow the lane round several sharp bends. On the higher ground join the South Downs Way and continue ahead.

Turn right before Buriton Farm **E** and follow the national trail as it heads north west. Avoid a path running down into woods on the right and a byway branching off left and continue on the South Downs Way. On reaching a junction with a footpath bearing right, turn left to continue on the trail. Begin a moderate climb over the South Downs. At a fork, just before a National Trust sign for Harting Downs, keep right and climb steeply. Take either path at the first fork and then the left one at the second to reach a toposcope and trig point on Beacon Hill.

At almost 800 feet, this is one of the highest points on the South Downs. The hill fort on its summit is rectangular and extends to 40 feet. Five Bronze axe-heads, thought to be part of a merchant's hoard, were discovered here. During the Napoleonic Wars there was a semaphore station on Beacon Hill; the station was one of a chain, which conveyed messages between Whitehall and nearby Portsmouth.

Descend steeply and as you do so, look for a fork farther down. Keep right on reaching it and head for a wooden waymark with a flint and stone base **F**. Go through a galvanised gate and up the track, still following the South Downs Way. Gradually South Harting and its church edge into view. Pass through a gate into a meadow, follow the path through it and soon the car park is seen ahead. ●

On Beacon Hill

West Hoathly and Weir Wood Reservoir

		GPS waypoints
Start	West Hoathly	
Distance	8 miles (12.9km)	TQ 366 325
Height gain	900 feet (275m)	**A** TQ 364 330
Approximate time	4 hours	**B** TQ 362 341
Parking	Finchefield car park, to the east of the village	**C** TQ 372 347
		D TQ 382 360
Route terrain	Undulating paths and tracks through thickly wooded country	**E** TQ 388 349
		F TQ 379 340
Ordnance Survey maps	Landranger 198 (Brighton & Lewes), Explorer 135 (Ashdown Forest)	**G** TQ 371 332

The whistle of steam trains on the nearby Bluebell Railway and the muffled roar of aircraft landing and taking off at Gatwick highlight the contrast between two very different modes of transport on this lovely walk, which follows sections of two popular trails – the High Weald Landscape Trail and the Sussex Border Path. History, architecture and wildlife add an extra dimension to the proceedings with a visit to Standen, a National Trust property, and a stroll along the banks of Weir Wood Reservoir.

Close to the start of the walk, in the centre of West Hoathly, stands a timber-framed hall house built in the 15th century for the Priory of St Pancras in Lewes. The Priest House was seized by Henry VIII in 1538 and belonged at different times to Thomas Cromwell, Anne of Cleves, Mary I and Elizabeth I. Established as a museum in 1908, the Priest House includes a varied assortment of domestic bygones and items of 17th and 18th- century country furniture – among other features.

From the car park follow the path parallel to the road, keeping it on the left. Pass between a toposcope and a copse planted to commemorate the Coronation of King George VI in 1937.

Immediately before some steps leading down to the road, turn right at the footpath sign and cross the meadow to a gap in the fence. Keep ahead in the next field, down the slope to a gate in the trees. At the road turn left, following it up the slope for several hundred yards to the junction with North Lane. Keep right here **A**. Follow the public footpath to the left of a garage business and enter trees. Pass through a galvanised kissing-gate and shortly the path divides. Veer left on the High Weald Landscape Trail and down the field slope to a gap between holly bushes. Follow the path alongside a line of trees on the left with impressive views of Elizabethan Gravetye Manor, a

The Priest House at West Hoathly

luxury country house hotel, in the distance. Drop down to negotiate two stiles with a footpath running off to the left between them. Keep ahead to a kissing-gate on the edge of woodland and follow the High Weald Landscape Trail as it heads north. There is limited access here to adjacent Gravetye's Lower Lake as well as the Manor's public rooms and gardens.

Continue on the main path and on reaching a tarmac drive by the entrance to Gravetye Manor, keep right **B** and follow the drive. When it forks, veer right and follow the High Weald Landscape Trail to Home Farm. Pass the outbuildings and go straight on when the track divides in woodland. About 70 yds before reaching a tree-ringed field, bear right at a footpath sign. Cross a stream to a broad ride running beneath telegraph lines and a few paces beyond it turn right at an intersection. Follow the path to a tarmac lane and turn right. Steam trains on the Bluebell Railway rattle along the line to the left. Keep on

the lane as it sweeps round to the left and passes beneath the railway **C**. Pass Mill Place Farm and soon the track bends left and up between fields. Approach a house and take the path to the right of it. Pass through trees and then along the left edge of a field for about 100 yds. Swing left into woodland, pass alongside a track and continue on the path.

At a break in the trees, keep right at the waymark to a stile. Follow the path across the pasture for about 75 yds to a gap in the hedge and bracken and bear right in the next field towards trees. On reaching them bear left and follow the obvious path through the woods to a sports ground and playing fields. Continue ahead towards woodland on the far side and turn right alongside trees and wire fencing, following the path to the road. Turn right, pass Rockwood Park and then swing left at a bridleway **D**. Rejoin the High Weald Landscape Trail as it runs in from the left, skirt playing fields and follow the path through trees to the next road. Turn left for a few paces, then right by

a bus stop and sign for Standen.

The house is a Victorian family home with striking William Morris wallpapers and textiles and is the showpiece of the Arts and Craft Movement. Standen includes a formal hillside garden with superb views over the West and East Sussex border country. Approaching several houses, keep right at the waymark and follow the enclosed path to a wrought iron kissing-gate. Keep over to the left in the field, with glimpses of Standen in the distance. Avoid a path running in from the right and keep ahead on the path, now enclosed.

Pass a second path on the right, descend a bank and when the path forks, keep left through bracken and undergrowth. Follow the field edge to a stile **E** and turn right, following the Sussex Border Path alongside Weir Wood Reservoir, built in the early 1950s by damming the valley of the River Medway. Owned by Southern Water, the reservoir is 1½ miles long and covers 280 acres. Follow the trail and eventually reach the road. Turn left and

On the High Weald Landscape Trail

descend to the junction with Legsheath Lane. Cross it and go uphill, pass a footpath and a pair of cottages on the left and turn right at a stile and footpath **F**. Follow a sunken tree-lined path and drop down to a waymark and footbridge.

Keep right here, climb to a stile and follow an enclosed path across farmland. Merge with a concrete farm track and continue beyond the outbuildings to pass under the Bluebell Railway again. Follow the track round to the left **G** and keep ahead as far as Bluebell Lane on the right. Follow this bridleway, which narrows to a path and divides. Veer right and climb quite steeply to the road. Across the way is the **Intrepid Fox** pub. Cross the junction to the road signposted Hoathly church and climb steps to return to the car park. ●

Bosham and Fishbourne from West Itchenor

		GPS waypoints
Start	West Itchenor	
Distance	10 miles (16km)	✐ SU 798 012
Height gain	Negligible	Ⓐ SU 807 008
Approximate time	4½ hours	Ⓑ SU 815 005
Parking	At start	Ⓒ SU 826 010
Route terrain	Gentle waterside and farmland paths and tracks	Ⓓ SU 829 013
		Ⓔ SU 839 038
		Ⓕ SU 837 044
Ordnance Survey maps	Landranger 197 (Chichester & The South Downs), Explorer 120 (Chichester)	Ⓖ SU 829 034
		Ⓗ SU 801 031

This route is dependent on the ferry that crosses from Bosham to West Itchenor. It operates a daily service from mid-May until the end of September and at weekends and bank holidays from April until the end of October (Tel. 07970 378350). For times of tides call Chichester Harbour Conservancy on 01243 512301. It is best to avoid high tides. The end of the walk is a two-mile (3.2km) hike along the edge of the mudflats from Bosham Creek. Altogether this route makes a memorable day out.

✐ From the car park, walk to the main street and turn left. After 50 yds, opposite **The Ship Inn**, take the footpath on the right to Itchenor Sailing Club and turn right on to the shoreline path. Make the most of the river views as they last for only ¼ mile or so before splendid houses oblige the path to divert inland. Head for a residential drive and turn left. Follow the drive to signs for the Spinney and Woodsmoke. Head away from the river here Ⓐ, following the edge of the wood. After the copse continue ahead across farmland, avoid a path running in from the right and continue with the farm outbuildings on the left. On reaching a concrete farm drive, turn right.

The track becomes a lane. After 100 yds on this, turn left into Greenacres, ignore the right turning almost immediately and follow the drive to the right Ⓑ before leaving it to the left at the next bend, by a footpath sign. There is another brief stretch along the shoreline before the path strikes inland along the edge of a field with woodland to the left. When it joins a lane, keep ahead past a junction to pass Birdham Shipyard. Keep ahead past Birdham Pool but leave the lane by keeping ahead at a crossways Ⓒ on a path that turns left to cross the lock gates of Salterns Lock, the last lock of the Chichester Canal, an inland waterway that once linked London with Portsmouth. Walk by the side of the canal for 200 yds before turning left immediately before the

Marina Service Centre to head for the marina office. Cross the lock gate here (you may have to wait at busy times), pass the toilets and then turn immediately left towards the harbour. Turn right after a few paces to enter a copse, keeping left at the immediate fork ❿ to follow a permissive path through the copse and close to the shoreline with a distant view of Chichester Cathedral. Head inland around a property to reach a road and turn left to reach the **Crown and Anchor** pub at Dell Quay. Join the waterside path near the pub and follow it towards Fishbourne, avoiding paths on the right. Cross a channel and stay on the path along the flood bank to savour the wide views of sky and saltings even when a short-cut is offered to the right ❿.

Bear left after crossing a creek and cross a sparkling stream by footbridge and then a plank causeway over Fishbourne Meadows, which was part of the Roman harbour. *You can turn right at the end of the lane by the Mill ❿ if you want refreshment at the **Bull's Head**.* Alternatively, keep ahead across the lane on to the footpath that leads into a reedbed. Footbridges keep feet above the tide but at times the path is submerged by water. The path soon climbs above the reeds on to the flood wall on the west side of the harbour.

There are more views of Chichester Cathedral over the mud flats as you walk southwards. The path goes through strange woodland of stunted oak trees and passes a pond before swinging west, away from the river. At a T-junction ❿ turn right and then go left at the next junction. Pass alongside a line of trees and then cut between crops to reach Park Lane. Keep ahead on to an enclosed path, which is featureless but has the virtue of being straight. It swerves round an isolated cottage to

join its drive. The right of way leaves the drive when the latter bends left and then crosses two bridges. Continue on a field path and cross a lane to a house named 'Byways'. Pass the house to join an enclosed path and reach the head of Bosham Creek. The pubs and other delights of the village are to the right, the route continues to the left.

Follow Shore Road around the south side of the creek. Note that if the tide is

favourable you can take a short-cut across the mud on a causeway and stepping stones if you have visited the village. If the tide is high you may have to use the footpath to the left of the road.

After The Saltings the road swings away from the shore **H**. Keep ahead along the shoreline *(this is difficult when the tide is exceptionally high)*. The wonderful mix of sky and water, and the subdued colours of The Saltings make this particularly beautiful. Just when it seems that the ferry landing is mythical it comes into view, the causeway snaking over the mud. The trip across the river is a fitting end to the walk.   ●

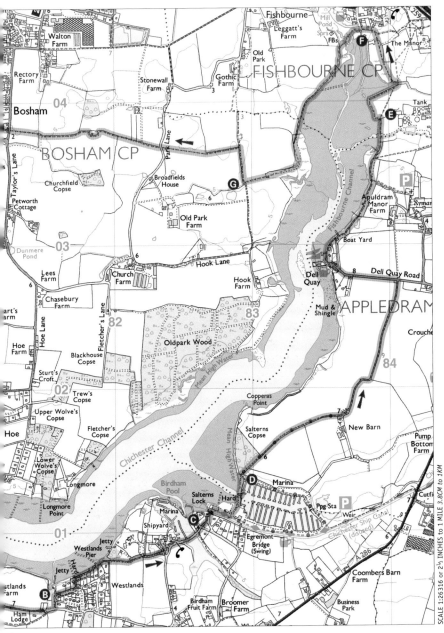

SCALE 1:26316 or 2⅓ INCHES to 1 MILE 3.8CM to 1KM

Goodwood and the West Sussex Literary Trail

		GPS waypoints
Start	Counter's Gate, Goodwood	
Distance	9½ miles (15.2km)	☑ SU 897 113
Height gain	1,065 feet (325m)	Ⓐ SU 888 129
		Ⓑ SU 891 139
Approximate time	4½ hours	Ⓒ SU 901 145
		Ⓓ SU 909 163
Parking	At start	Ⓔ SU 916 153
Route terrain	Lengthy stretches of track with	Ⓕ SU 907 139
	moderate climbing	Ⓖ SU 901 126
Ordnance Survey maps	Landranger 197 (Chichester & the South Downs), Explorers 120 (Chichester) and 121 (Arundel & Pulborough)	

One of Britain's most famous racecourses provides an unusual and entertaining backdrop to the initial stages of this glorious walk. Beyond the village of Charlton the route joins forces with the West Sussex Literary Trail and then a thickly wooded stretch of the South Downs Way. South of the charming village of East Dean, complete with duck pond and picture-postcard cottages, the walk meets a third long-distance trail – the popular Monarch's Way.

Goodwood is undoubtedly one of Britain's most famous and popular racecourses – thanks in no small measure to its superb position high on the South Downs. For one week every July it becomes 'Glorious Goodwood' when thousands of racegoers descend on this part of Sussex to attend one of the most prestigious events of the sporting and social calendar.

The course opened in 1801 after the Duke of Richmond gave part of his estate, Goodwood Park, to establish a track where members of the Goodwood Hunt Club and officers of the Sussex Militia could attend meetings. Towards the end of the 19th century, it acquired a rather unfortunate reputation when the rector of nearby Singleton protested

to the Chief Constable over the rowdy behaviour of racegoers. As a result, the crowds were restrained.

🖉 From the car park, head for the exit path in the corner and make for the road. Cross over to a junction of tracks. Bear left to join the bridleway and follow the track as it runs alongside Goodwood racecourse. Keep right at a fork and begin to descend through trees, with glimpses of the surrounding West Sussex countryside. Continue down to a gate, pass under some pylon cables and enter the village of Charlton.

The village is still remembered as the home of the Charlton Hunt. Among the huntsmen were the Duke of Richmond and a man named Tom Johnson, who became a legend in hunting circles.

The West Sussex Literary Trail

According to the mural tablet in Singleton church, 'he had no superior, and hardly an equal.' Established in the 18th century, the hunt's most notable chase took place on 28 January 1738. It began before 08.00 that morning and did not finish until 17.30! For about ten hours that day the fox led the pack a merry dance in the fields and woods between Charlton and East Dean. Eventually, the hounds cornered their prey, an elderly vixen, close to the River Arun.

On the right is a striking war memorial recalling the fallen comrades of the Sussex Yeomanry. Keep right at the fork here, pass a telephone box and at the T-junction, opposite the **Fox Goes Free** pub, turn left **Ⓐ**. Pass the **Woodstock House Hotel** and take the next right into North Lane. The lane dwindles to a stony track and passes Ware Barn. At the next fork **Ⓑ**, swing right to follow the path signposted West Sussex Literary Trail.

Climb steeply up the bank and keep ahead at the top with trees and bushes to the right. Continue to a stile and opening into the next field and after about 50 yds you join a track. Keep right here and shortly you reach a footpath sign with another visible in the field. At this point line up the two posts and go diagonally across the pasture towards woodland. Make for a stile and follow the path through the trees to a clearing where the path merges with a track running in from the left. Continue ahead. Follow the grassy path down to a major intersection; avoid the immediate left turning and at the fork in front of you, take the left exit into the trees **Ⓒ**. Keep ahead through the woods, merge with a bridleway and continue to the next junction, which is waymarked. Continue ahead on the West Sussex Literary Trail but now on a broader track running between trees. Follow the straight track as it rises gently, cross the Broad Walk and soon you reach the South Downs Way **Ⓓ**.

Turn right here to follow a broad ride, pass a junction with a restricted byway on the left and keep going on the long-distance trail. The Broad Walk is glimpsed on the right through the trees. Immediately beyond a gate leading to Bowleys Field on the left, turn sharp right on to a bridleway. After about 100 yds, cross over a track and continue all the way down through the woods to their southern edge, where there is a very pleasant view of a tree-ringed field rippling away below you **E**. As you descend through the field, look a little to the right and the buildings of Goodwood, including the grandstand, can be glimpsed on the skyline. On reaching a footpath and bridleway sign at the foot of the slope,

The village pond at East Dean

turn right on to a cycle track. Follow it almost to Postles Barn and swing sharp left at the gate to join a bridleway running up the edge of the field to a second gate. Follow the track up through the trees, with Postles Barn seen below to the right.

Follow the track to a waymarked junction of bridleways and head straight on, still between trees. Farther on, descend on a sunken path and emerge finally into open farmland. Follow the obvious path down to a lane and turn left **F**. Pass the buildings of New Barn and continue on the lane towards East Dean. The 12th century church of All Saints is seen on the right as you enter the village. Walk down Newhouse Lane to the junction and turn right. Pass the **Star & Garter** pub and when the road bends right by the pond, swing left at the sign for Goodwood and Chichester. Pass Manor Farmhouse and continue up the lane to a footpath on the right just before a sign for East Dean for oncoming traffic **G**. Following the Monarch's Way, walk through the trees to a gateway and stile. Keep along the right-hand edge of the field and look for a stile. Bear left in the next pasture and climb quite steeply towards woodland. Head for a stile and gateway

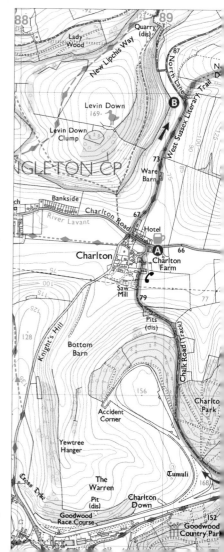

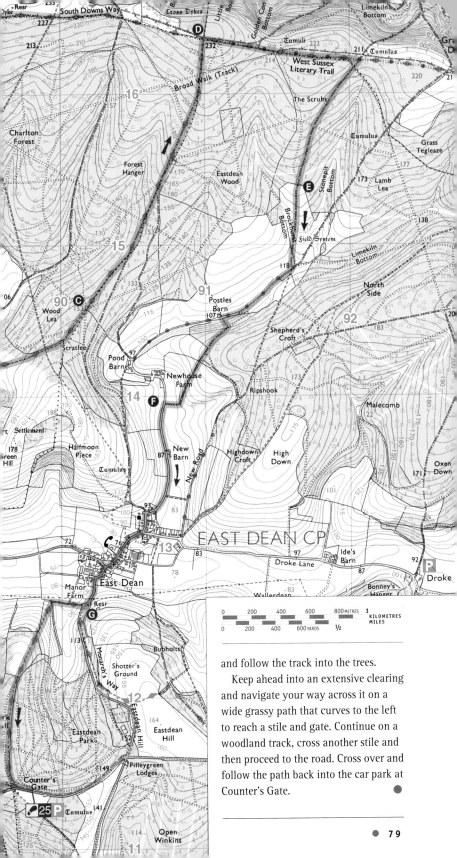

and follow the track into the trees.

Keep ahead into an extensive clearing and navigate your way across it on a wide grassy path that curves to the left to reach a stile and gate. Continue on a woodland track, cross another stile and then proceed to the road. Cross over and follow the path back into the car park at Counter's Gate.

Bramber, Beeding and the Downs Link

Start	Bramber Castle	**GPS waypoints**	
Distance	11 miles (17.6km)	🖉 TQ 185 106	
Height gain	295 feet (90m)	Ⓐ TQ 192 106	
Approximate time	5 hours	Ⓑ TQ 201 134	
Parking	At start	Ⓒ TQ 209 136	
Route terrain	Riverside and field paths, lengthy section of disused railway	Ⓓ TQ 213 152	
		Ⓔ TQ 206 161	
Ordnance Survey maps	Landranger 198 (Brighton & Lewes), Explorer 122 (Brighton & Hove)	Ⓕ TQ 199 136	

The crumbling remains of one of the county's most famous and historic strongholds provides the setting for the start of this fascinating and very varied walk, which begins by following the River Adur upstream for several miles. The next leg is over fields and meadows to the walk's halfway point – the bustling village of Henfield, with its high street pubs and local museum. From here the walk turns south, following the popular Downs Link, formerly two branch railway lines, back to the start.

The strategic importance of Bramber Castle was crucial. It was built soon after the Norman Conquest on ancient earthworks to defend the open and exposed Sussex coast – specifically what is known as the Adur Gap. The de Braose family held Bramber Castle until 1326 when it passed to Alice de Bohun and then to her eldest son. Later, at the height of the Civil War, it was badly attacked by the Roundheads. These days, all that remains is the 70 feet (21m)-high gateway.

The adjoining parish church of St Nicholas was originally the castle chapel and was probably built late in the 11th century by William de Braose. Like the castle, the church also suffered in battle. Cromwell's men apparently used it as a gun emplacement, causing extensive damage to the nave and tower.

🖉 Start the walk in the car park below Bramber Castle ruins, avoid the vehicular exit to the road and take the path to the right of the Norman church. Go down beside the lychgate to the village street. Opposite is the **Old Tollgate Hotel and Restaurant**. Keep left through Bramber, pass public conveniences and follow the road to St Mary's House. This medieval building includes the best example of late 15th-century timber framing in Sussex and also contains the unique printed room decorated for the visit of Elizabeth I. Continue into Upper Beeding, cross Beeding Bridge and turn left opposite the **Bridge** pub Ⓐ to follow the riverside path. Charles II crossed this

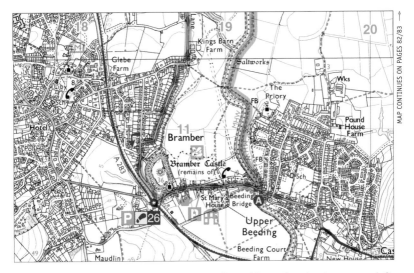

bridge in 1651 as a fugitive on the run. Pursued by Parliamentary forces, the King was making his way to Shoreham, en route to France.

Pass through a kissing-gate and head up river directly beside the Adur. The river here was once a broad estuary with boats reaching the port of Steyning. Visible along this stretch are the remnants of the old salt industry that thrived on the mud flats before the ground level rose by about three metres. Go through a second kissing-gate, avoid the footbridge and continue up river to cross a series of stiles. Pass beneath

By the Adur

pylon cables and as the river curves left towards a bridge, turn right to join a footpath, crossing a footbridge **B**. Follow the field edge on a grassy track, passing under the pylon cables to reach the entrance to Stretham Manor. Keep ahead on the tarmac drive, pass Stretham Farm House and a waymarked track and follow the farm road as it bears left.

Turn left at the next footpath sign **C** and follow the field edge with the boundary on the right. Cross a stile and turn right to the corner of the pasture. Avoid the stile ahead; instead, turn left at the waymark and keep fencing on the right. Pass into the next field and aim

for its far right-hand corner. Go through a gate into the next pasture and keep ahead on a path through a strip of woodland. If overgrown, follow the field edge, keeping trees to the right. On reaching a gate and stile, cross a track and go straight ahead up the field, keeping hedge and light woodland to the left. Make for a gate in the hedge and in the next pasture drop down the slope to a kissing-gate in the boundary. Beyond a track and stile, cross a meadow to a footbridge by a waymark **D**.

Pass through scrubby vegetation to the next stile and footpath junction. Head straight on, following the grassy uphill path between fields and join a track in the top corner. Follow it ahead to the A2037, cross Neptown Road and follow the pavement ahead into Henfield. Walk down the High Street; turn right into Coopers Way to visit the Henfield Museum and afterwards continue along the main street, turning left opposite **the White Hart** into Church Street. Cross Chestnut Way and Parsonage Road to follow a stretch of pavement set back from the road. Pass Church Lane and continue along Upper Station Road to the **Cat and Canary** pub. Turn left into Station Road **E** and walk down to a junction with Hollands Lane.

Turn right here, then almost immediately left at the sign for Downs Link, a 37-mile (59km) waymarked trail linking the North Downs Way with the South Downs Way. Much of it follows the course of two dismantled railways – the Cranleigh line and the Steyning line. Follow the disused railway between hedgerows, with glimpses of the South Downs here and there. Cross a footpath by a cottage and at length the trail reaches a suitably placed seat offering good views across lazy meadows to distant downland. Cross a small bridge, pass a path on the left and then

a waymark. Stretham Manor edges into view on the left now, glimpsed through the trees. Cross the River Adur **F** and continue on the Downs Link over two more bridges before leaving the old trackbed to sweep round to the right.

Avoid a footpath running along the field edge at this point and follow the track across farmland to a T-junction by galvanised gates. Turn left, still following the Downs Link, and pass the outbuildings of Wyckham Farm, many of them converted. Proceed past several more farms and a radio transmitter and around several bends to reach a T-junction. Turn left to the junction of Roman Road and Castle Lane. Go straight on here, following the lane ahead through trees with the remains of Bramber Castle up to the left. At the next road junction turn left, back to the car park.   ●

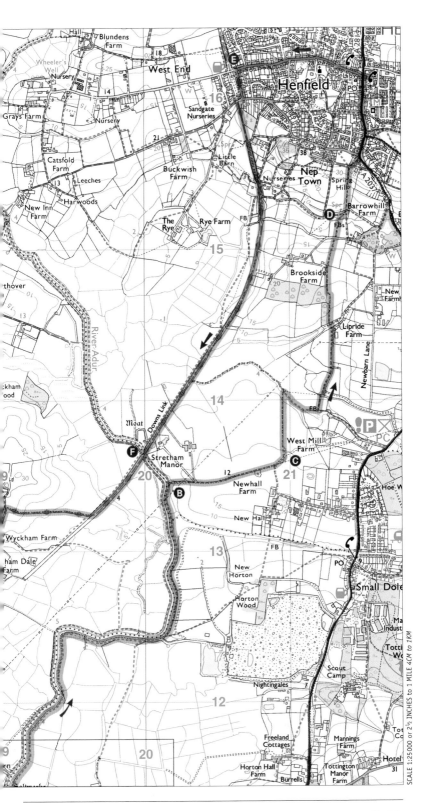

Cissbury and Chanctonbury Rings

Cissbury and Chanctonbury Rings

		GPS waypoints	
Start	Findon Valley. Follow the A24 north of Worthing and the junction with the A27. Turn right into Lime Tree Avenue immediately before a row of shops and fork right, up Coombe Rise to the car park	🖉 TQ 133 066	
		Ⓐ TQ 139 067	
		Ⓑ TQ 139 085	
		Ⓒ TQ 151 083	
		Ⓓ TQ 151 097	
Distance	11 miles (17.6km)	Ⓔ TQ 162 099	
Height gain	1,360 feet (415m)	Ⓕ TQ 139 120	
Approximate time	5½ hours	Ⓖ TQ 121 103	
Parking	Coombe Rise car park	Ⓗ TQ 138 093	
Route terrain	Mainly undulating downland paths and tracks		
Ordnance Survey maps	Landranger 198 (Brighton & Lewes), Explorer 121 (Arundel & Pulborough)		

This lengthy walk of broad and sweeping vistas not only embraces some of the grandest scenery on the South Downs but also passes two of the finest prehistoric hill forts – Cissbury Ring and Chanctonbury Ring. Although there are several climbs, these are all long and gradual.

🖉 Begin by taking the uphill track from the car park, at a fork keep along the right-hand path, and continue uphill to a

Looking from Cissbury Ring towards the circle of beeches that crown Chanctonbury Ring

T-junction of paths Ⓐ. Turn left along a pleasantly hedge– and tree-lined path, eventually emerging into open country, with a fine view of Cissbury Ring straight ahead. Go through a gate before reaching a National Trust sign for Cissbury Ring and a fence. Keep along the left-hand edge of a copse lined by some fine old trees.

On reaching a kissing-gate continue ahead to pass through the ramparts of this huge fort, one of the greatest of Iron Age hill forts, enclosing

En route to Cissbury Ring

an area of 65 acres. The inner bank has a circumference of over one mile. Built around 300 BC, the fort was deserted sometime between 50 BC and AD 50 but reinforced and reoccupied after the departure of the Romans; whether this was done by the Saxons or by the Britons as a defence against the Saxons is uncertain.

Continue along a broad grassy track across the middle of the site and when the track forks, keep left to reach a triangulation pillar (604 feet) and viewpoint. Walk back 100 yds and take the grassy path on the right. Follow it downhill, pass over the ramparts and go down some steps to cross a track. Continue ahead to the next gate **B**. Go through the gate, turn right along a broad stony track which heads gently downhill and continue, between wire fences, to a gate **C**.

Here turn left along a track that winds through Stump Bottom and at a T-junction **D** turn right onto a path that at first heads steadily uphill and later flattens out. Continue to a crossing of paths and tracks; here turn left to join the South Downs Way **E**. Follow it gently uphill for two miles, ignoring all side turns, to Chanctonbury Ring **F**, another Iron Age fort but much smaller than Cissbury Ring. It is easily distinguished by its circle of beeches, planted in the 1760s by Charles Goring, a local landowner, which gives the fort an air of mystery, especially in misty conditions. In clear weather there is a magnificent view across the wide, empty expanses of the downs looking southwards towards Cissbury Ring and the coast.

Continue along the South Downs Way, passing below the triangulation pillar on Chanctonbury Hill – 780 feet high and another superb viewpoint – and to the left of a restored dew pond, first made in around 1870 to provide water for animals. Head gently downhill and where the South Downs Way turns right keep straight ahead, continuing downhill all the while. At a crossing of tracks turn left **Ⓖ**, continuing downhill at first but soon starting to head uphill. Look out for a gate and bridleway arrow on the right.

Keep in a straight line across a field to go through a metal gate onto a lane, cross over, go through a gate opposite and continue gently uphill across the next field, keeping in the same direction as before, to a gate. Go through it to a crossing of tracks, turn left and pass to the left of a house, after which the track narrows to a hedge—and tree-lined path. Continue along it, keeping ahead at the first public bridleway sign, but at a T-junction bear left onto a broad track.

Continue along this track for about 100 yds, passing a waymark and gate and turning right **Ⓗ** at a crossing of tracks.

Chanctonbury Ring

The track leads straight to Cissbury Ring where you pick up the outward route **Ⓑ** and retrace your steps through the fort back to the start. ●

Bignor Hill and the River Arun

		GPS waypoints
Start	Summit of Bignor Hill	🥾 SU 973 129
Distance	Option 1: 11½ miles (18.4km) Option 2: 8½ miles (13.5km) Option 3: 5 miles (8km)	Ⓐ SU 989 132 Ⓑ TQ 000 119 Ⓒ TQ 025 118
Height gain	1: 1,230 feet (375m); 2: 1,180 feet (360m); 3: 605 feet (185m)	Ⓓ TQ 025 099 Ⓔ TQ 018 112
Approximate time	Option 1: 5½ hours. Option 2: 4½ hours Option 3: 2½ hours	Ⓕ TQ 001 110 Ⓖ SU 996 112
Parking	At start	Ⓗ SU 988 113
Route terrain	Fine mix of downland tracks and meandering riverside paths	
Ordnance Survey maps	Landranger 197 (Chichester & The South Downs), Explorer 121 (Arundel & Pulborough)	

This varied and flexible route offers something for everyone. All the walks include woodland trails and an invigorating stretch of the South Downs Way. Options 1 and 2 both feature attractive sections beside the River Arun, while the longest route also passes the delightful little church at South Stoke. There are no refreshment stops on Option 3.

The surfaced road to Bignor Hill ends at the parking area, where the signpost underlines the significance of the hill to the Romans by pointing in the direction of Londinium and Noviomagus (Chichester).

🥾 Turn back down the road towards Londinium but fork right away from the road and climb the flinty track to the summit of Bignor Hill on the South Downs Way. There are wonderful views as the track leaves National Trust land.

Keep on the South Downs Way as it descends and swings left to come to a crossways below Westburton Hill Ⓐ.

Bear right past the cattle shed to follow the South Downs Way as it climbs steadily along the side of Westburton Hill towards woodland. About a mile farther on, the path divides at a copse on the right Ⓑ.

Turn right at the bridleway sign for Whiteways to follow Option 3 heading due south along the edge of Langham Wood to rejoin the longer route at Ⓕ.

Otherwise, keep straight on along the main track as the A29 comes into view ahead. Turn right onto the main road and, after about 80 yds, cross it to a continuation of the South Downs Way – a track that descends steeply with Coombe Wood to the left. At the end of the wood the river comes into view with Bury church to the left, one of the most memorable of Downland panoramas.

Cross the road at the bottom and

Cyclists on the South Downs Way

follow the South Downs Way to cross the graceful bridge. Turn right along the north bank of the River Arun and stay on the riverbank path when the South Downs Way leaves to the left. The path skirts a residential caravan site before reaching a road at Amberley. Turn right to pass the **Bridge Inn**, the **Riverside Café** and the **Boathouse Brasserie** and head out onto Houghton Bridge **C**.

To follow Option 2, cross the bridge and turn immediately left at a gate onto the riverside footpath; this section may be boggy in wet weather. After ½ mile turn right to rejoin the longer route at **E**.

Just halfway across the bridge, the main route turns left onto an islet and follows the southern riverbank for 650 yds before coming to a footbridge across a dyke. Cross a stile here and follow the path away from the river.

In places it is narrow and somewhat overgrown with brambles and roses. Turn right when you reach Stoke Road and follow the lane to a T-junction at North Stoke. Go left at the telephone box and then immediately right on to a field path that heads south towards South Stoke and passes through three kissing-gates. Cross a delightful little suspension bridge repaired and restored in 2009 by 70 Gurkha Field Support Squadron, the Queen's Gurkha Engineers. The path at length emerges on to the lovely riverbank near the bridge at South Stoke. Cross the bridge and climb past St Leonard's Church with its spire, which would seem more at home on a bank of the Rhine than the Arun.

Take the bridleway to the right from the lane immediately after South Stoke Farm **D**, where the stables are in the same style as the church. Pass the back of this building and then turn left on to a bridleway above the river. There is a

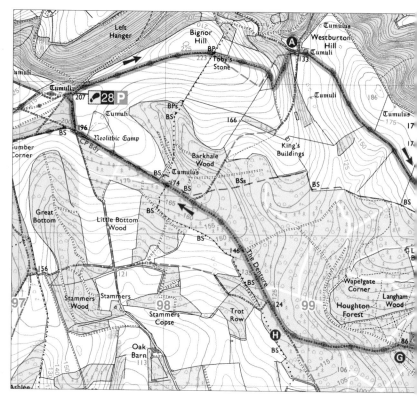

steep climb along the edge of a field with a fine view at the top.

The path is well above the river for much of the way to Houghton with Arundel Park wall to the left. A kissing-gate brings another footpath to join the riverside path (this is the Monarch's Way, named to celebrate Charles II's flight through Sussex to exile in France). Beware of exposed tree roots where the path is squeezed between wall and river. The river is invariably muddy, and it would be dangerous to swim in it. There is a clearing with a chalky cliff face above, which is a popular place for a barbecue. About 100 yds before a gate, a waymark and a house, pass a path on the right.

E *Option 2 rejoins the main walk here.*

When the path meets a lane, climb it to the main road and turn left to pass the **George and Dragon**, where King Charles is said to have stopped for a pint or two. Take the private road that branches to the right just beyond the pub but, after 20 yds, follow the 'walkers' sign on to a bridleway between the drive and the road. This climbs steadily and crosses another drive before becoming a field-edge path giving fine views to the left over the valley. The gradient eases, and the path becomes enclosed and passes close to a car park. At the end of a long section of woodland walking you emerge to cross a field to the A29.

Cross the main road to continue on the bridleway ahead keeping right. When the path swings to the right and starts to climb steeply, leave it to the left **F**.

Option 3 rejoins the main walk here.

Walk down a short length of well-used track to reach a broad cycleway. Turn right on to this right of way, which descends gently.

G Fork left 50 yds after the 'Please respect other users' notice, and then cross another track.

Now the path begins to climb more seriously. When it levels out another bridleway joins from the left **H**, and there is pleasant walking on a broad, grassy, straight track that climbs gently past yet another bridleway on the left. Now settle into your stride for a mile of steady climbing. The view opens up on the right as you pass a National Trust sign, and the gradient finally eases at a crossways with a wide vista on your left. Turn right here, keeping the woods on your left, to climb the final 300 yds to the car park.

Further Information

Walking Safety

Although the reasonably gentle countryside that is the subject of this book offers no real dangers to walkers at any time of the year, it is still advisable to take sensible precautions and follow certain well-tried guidelines.

Always take with you both warm and waterproof clothing and sufficient food and drink. Wear suitable footwear, such as strong walking boots or shoes that give a good grip over stony ground, on slippery slopes and in muddy conditions. Try to obtain a local weather forecast and bear it in mind before you start. Do not be afraid to abandon your proposed route and return to your starting point in the event of a sudden and unexpected deterioration in the weather.

All the walks described in this book will be safe to do, given due care and respect, even during the winter. Indeed, a crisp, fine winter day often provides perfect walking conditions, with firm ground underfoot and a clarity unique to this time of the year. The most difficult hazard likely to be encountered is mud, especially when walking along woodland and field paths, farm tracks and bridleways – the latter in particular can often get churned up by cyclists and horses. In summer, an additional difficulty may be narrow and overgrown paths, particularly along the edges of cultivated fields. Neither should constitute a major problem provided that the appropriate footwear is worn.

The Ramblers' Association

No organisation works more actively to protect and extend the rights and interests of walkers in the countryside than the Ramblers' Association. Its aims are clear: to foster a greater knowledge, love and care of the countryside; to assist in the protection and enhancement of public rights of way and areas of natural beauty; to work for greater public access to the countryside; and to encourage more people to take up rambling as a healthy, recreational leisure activity.

It was founded in 1935 and then Ramblers' Association has played a key role in preserving and developing the national footpath network, supporting the creation of national parks and encouraging the designation and waymarking of long-distance routes.

Our freedom of access to the countryside, now enshrined in legislation, is still in its early years and requires constant vigilance. But over and above this there will always be the problem of footpaths being illegally obstructed, disappearing through lack of use, or being extinguished by housing or road construction.

It is to meet such problems and dangers that the Ramblers' Association exists and represents the interests of all walkers. The address to write to for information on the Ramblers' Association and how to become a member is given on page 95.

Walkers and the Law

The Countryside and Rights of Way Act (CRoW Act 2000) extends the rights of access previously enjoyed by walkers in England and Wales. Implementation of these rights began on 19 September 2004. The Act amends existing legislation and for the first time provides access on foot to certain types of land – defined as mountain, moor, heath, down and registered common land.

Where You Can Go
Rights of Way
Prior to the introduction of the CRoW Act, walkers could only legally access the countryside along public rights of way. These are either 'footpaths' (for walkers only) or 'bridleways' (for walkers, riders on horseback and pedal cyclists). A third category called 'Byways open to all traffic'

Countryside Access Charter

Your rights of way are:

- public footpaths – on foot only. Sometimes waymarked in yellow
- bridle-ways – on foot, horseback and pedal cycle. Sometimes waymarked in blue
- byways (usually old roads), most 'roads used as public paths' and, of course, public roads – all traffic has the right of way

Use maps, signs and waymarks to check rights of way. Ordnance Survey Explorer and Landranger maps show most public rights of way

On rights of way you can:

- take a pram, pushchair or wheelchair if practicable
- take a dog (on a lead or under close control)
- take a short route round an illegal obstruction or remove it sufficiently to get past

You have a right to go for recreation to:

- public parks and open spaces – on foot
- most commons near older towns and cities – on foot and sometimes on horseback
- private land where the owner has a formal agreement with the local authority

In addition you can use the following by local or established custom or consent, but ask for advice if you are unsure:

- many areas of open country, such as moorland, fell and coastal areas, especially those in the care of the National Trust, and some commons
- some woods and forests, especially those owned by the Forestry Commission
- country parks and picnic sites
- most beaches
- canal towpaths
- some private paths and tracks Consent sometimes extends to horse-riding and cycling

For your information:

- county councils and London boroughs maintain and record rights of way, and register commons
- obstructions, dangerous animals, harassment and misleading signs on rights of way are illegal and you should report them to the county council
- paths across fields can be ploughed, but must normally be reinstated within two weeks
- landowners can require you to leave land to which you have no right of access
- motor vehicles are normally permitted only on roads, byways and some 'roads used as public paths'

(BOATs), is used by motorised vehicles as well as those using non-mechanised transport. Mainly they are green lanes, farm and estate roads, although occasionally they will be found crossing mountainous area.

Rights of way are marked on Ordnance Survey maps. Look for the green broken lines on the Explorer maps, or the red dashed lines on Landranger maps.

The term 'right of way' means exactly what it says. It gives a right of passage over what, for the most part, is private land. Under pre-CRoW legislation walkers were required to keep to the line of the right of way and not stray onto land on either side. If you did inadvertently wander off the right of way, either because of faulty map reading or because the route was not clearly indicated on the ground, you were technically trespassing.

Local authorities have a legal obligation to ensure that rights of way are kept clear and free of obstruction, and are signposted where they leave metalled roads. The duty of local authorities to install signposts extends to the placing of signs along a path or way, but only where the authority considers it necessary to have a signpost or waymark to assist persons unfamiliar with the locality.

The New Access Rights
Access Land

As well as being able to walk on existing rights of way, under the new legislation you now have access to large areas of open land. You can of course continue to use rights of way footpaths to cross this land, but the main difference is that you can now lawfully leave the path and wander at will, but only in areas designated as access land.

Where to Walk

Areas now covered by the new access rights – Access Land – are shown on Ordnance Survey Explorer maps bearing the access land symbol on the front cover.

'Access Land' is shown on Ordnance Survey maps by a light yellow tint surrounded by a pale orange border. New orange coloured 'i' symbols on the maps will show the location of permanent access information boards installed by the access authorities.

Restrictions

The right to walk on access land may lawfully be restricted by landowners. Landowners can, for any reason, restrict access for up to 28 days in any year. They cannot however close the land:

- on bank holidays;
- for more than four Saturdays and Sundays in a year;
- on any Saturday from 1 June to 11 August; or
- on any Sunday from 1 June to the end of September.

They have to provide local authorities with five working days' notice before the date of closure unless the land involved is an area of less than five hectares or the closure is for less than four hours. In these cases landowners only need to provide two hours' notice.

Whatever restrictions are put into place on access land they have no effect on existing rights of way, and you can continue to walk on them.

Dogs

Dogs can be taken on access land, but must be kept on leads of two metres or less between 1 March and 31 July, and at all times where they are near livestock. In addition landowners may impose a ban on all dogs from fields where lambing takes place for up to six weeks in any year. Dogs may be banned from moorland used for grouse shooting and breeding for up to five years.

In the main, walkers following the routes in this book will continue to follow existing rights of way, but a knowledge and understanding of the law as it affects walkers, plus the ability to distinguish access land marked on the maps, will enable anyone who wishes to depart from paths that cross access land either to take a shortcut, to enjoy a view or to explore.

General Obstructions

Obstructions can sometimes cause a problem on a walk and the most common of these is where the path across a field has been ploughed over. It is legal for a farmer to plough up a path provided that it is restored within two weeks. This does not always happen and you are faced with the dilemma of following the line of the path, even if this means treading on crops, or walking round the edge of the field. Although the latter course of action seems the most sensible, it does mean that you would be trespassing.

Other obstructions can vary from overhanging vegetation to wire fences across the path, locked gates or even a cattle feeder on the path.

Use common sense. If you can get round the obstruction without causing damage, do so. Otherwise only remove as much of the obstruction as is necessary to secure passage.

If the right of way is blocked and cannot be followed, there is a long-standing view that in such circumstances there is a right to deviate, but this cannot wholly be relied on. Although it is accepted in law that highways (and that includes rights of way) are for the public service, and if the usual track is impassable, it is for the general good that people should be entitled to pass into another line. However, this should not be taken as indicating a right to deviate whenever a way becomes impassable. If in doubt, retreat.

Report obstructions to the local authority and/or The Ramblers.

Useful Organisations

Campaign to Protect Rural England
128 Southwark St, London SE1 0SW
Tel. 020 7981 2800
www.cpre.org.uk

English Heritage
Customer Services, PO Box 569
Swindon SN2 2YP
Tel. 0870 3331181
www.english-heritage.org.uk

National Trust
Membership and General Enquiries
PO Box 39, Warrington
WA5 7WD
Tel. 08704 4584000
www.nationaltrust.org.uk

Natural England
John Dower House, Crescent Place
Cheltenham GL50 3RA
Tel. 0300 060 2481
www.naturalengland.org.uk

Ordnance Survey
Romsey Road, Maybush,
SouthamptonSO16 4GU
Tel. 08456 050505 (lo-call)
www.ordnancesurvey.co.uk

Ramblers' Association
2nd Floor, Camelford House
87-90 Albert Embankment,
London SE1 7TW
Tel. 020 7339 8500
www.ramblers.org.uk

Youth Hostels Association
Trevelyan House, Dimple Road, Matlock
Derbyshire DE4 3YH
Tel. 01629 592600
www.yha.org.uk

Traveline
Tel. 0871 200 2233

National Train Enquiry Line
Tel. 0845 484950

Tourist Information Centres
Arundel: 01903 882268
Bognor Regis: 01243 823140
Brighton & Hove: 0906 711 2255
Chichester: 01243 775888
Horsham: 01403 211661
Littlehampton: 01903 721866
Midhurst: 01730 817322/815933
Worthing: 01903 210022/221394

West Sussex County Council
County Hall, West Street,
Chichester
West Sussex
PO19 1RQ
Tel. 01243 777100
www.westsussex.gov.uk

Ordnance Survey maps of West Sussex & the South Downs

West Sussex and the South Downs are covered by Ordnance Survey 1:50 000 scale (1$\frac{1}{4}$ inches to 1 mile or 2cm to 1km) Landranger map sheets 186, 187, 197, and 198. These all-purpose maps are packed with information to help you explore the area. Viewpoints, picnic sites, places of interest and caravan and camping sites are shown, as well as public rights of way information such as footpaths and bridleways. To examine West Sussex and the South Downs in more detail, and especially if you are planning walks, Ordnance Survey Explorer maps at 1:25 000 (2$\frac{1}{2}$ inches to 1 mile or 4cm to 1km) are ideal:

120 Chichester
121 Arundel & Pulborough
122 Brighton & Hove
133 Haslemere & Petersfield
134 Crawley & Horsham
135 Ashdown Forest

To get to West Sussex and the South Downs, use the Ordnance Survey Travel Map-Route Great Britain at 1:625 000 (1 inch to 10 miles or 4cm to 25km) scale.

Ordnance Survey maps and guides are available from most booksellers, stationers and newsagents.

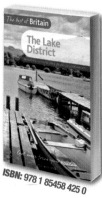